FOUNDATIONS OF STATE AND LOCAL GOVERNMENT SERIES

WALLACE S. SAYRE, *Editor*

POLITICS OF POLICY
Alan K. Campbell

URBAN POLITICAL SYSTEMS
Demetrios Caraley

STATE LEGISLATIVE SYSTEMS
Wilder Crane, Jr. and *Meredith W. Watts, Jr.*

STATE POLITICAL SYSTEMS
H. Douglas Price

STATE JUDICIAL SYSTEMS
Kenneth N. Vines

STATE EXECUTIVE SYSTEMS
York Willbern

Additional titles to be announced.

WILDER CRANE, JR.
The University of Wisconsin-Milwaukee

MEREDITH W. WATTS, JR.
The University of Wisconsin-Milwaukee

STATE

LEGISLATIVE

SYSTEMS

Prentice-Hall, Inc., Englewood Cliffs, New Jersey

PRENTICE-HALL INTERNATIONAL, INC. *London*
PRENTICE-HALL OF AUSTRALIA, PTY. LTD. *Sydney*
PRENTICE-HALL OF CANADA, LTD. *Toronto*
PRENTICE-HALL OF INDIA PRIVATE LTD. *New Delhi*
PRENTICE-HALL OF JAPAN, INC. *Tokyo*

Printed in the United States of America

Library of Congress Catalog Card No. 68-15907

Current printing (last number):
10 9 8 7 6 5 4 3 2 1

FOUNDATIONS OF STATE AND LOCAL GOVERNMENT SERIES

State and local governments, and the political processes which animate them, have undergone a great
transformation in the past quarter century. The rapid
pace of urbanization in the United States; the rise of
metropolitanization; the entry of the national government into complex and expanding partnership
arrangements with state and local governments in
conceiving, financing and administering social and
economic programs of great variety; the identification of new and urgent priorities involving state and
local government performance; the increasing pressures upon these governments to modernize their
organizational capacities to meet multiplied demands
—all these and other forces have radically modified
the traditional bases of state and local political
processes. These developments have imposed new
and major burdens upon those who study state and
local government and politics in the United States.
Particularly do those who teach these subjects in
colleges and universities find it difficult to discover
satisfactory analyses designed for the classroom,
materials which will appraise the effects of widespread governmental change upon the institutions
and processes of politics at state and local levels.
    The aim of the Foundations of State and Local
Government Series is to provide a set of texts that will
meet these needs. Social scientists generally and

political scientists especially have recently developed extensive descriptions and explanations of the profound changes in state and local politics, but these materials are so widely scattered in the professional literature that it is difficult to find ways to use them in the classroom. The authors of this series are alert and sensitive to the values of these new sources of data, new methods of inquiry, and new insights. Recognized experts in their particular subjects, they use the flexibility and freedom of the series to present their separate areas with fullness and recency. Each volume, complete in itself, is intended to complement the others. Taken together, they constitute a well-rounded, full-length text. Separately, they are pertinent collateral readings or supplements to another textbook. Comprehensive but concise, with unifying threads of an integrated approach for the series as a whole, the volumes offer a broad new choice for the instructor. He can, as he wishes, combine them into a text of his own design in sequence or emphasis—full-length or brief, as he, himself, prefers.

The first volume of the series, Wilder Crane's and Meredith Watts's *State Legislative Systems*, appraises the new forces affecting state legislative institutions, their adaptations to these strong influences, and the continuing dilemmas of the legislative process. In the volumes that follow, H. Douglas Price describes *State Political Systems* comparatively, applying the most recent analytical concepts and methods to the changing politics of the fifty states; and Demetrios Caraley similarly portrays the *Urban Political Systems* of the United States, appraising the impact of rising urbanization and metropolitanization on the government and politics of cities.

Alan K. Campbell deals with the *Politics of Policy* in state and local government, emphasizing especially the processes of resource allocation by state and local political systems. Kenneth N. Vines analyses *State Judicial Systems*, relating state and local judiciary to the political systems within which the courts operate; and York Willbern, in *State Executive Systems*, describes analytically and comparatively the developing roles and functions of the governors, the executive agencies, and the bureaucracies of state governments.

WALLACE S. SAYRE

CONTENTS

I INTRODUCTION
page 1

Historical Trends in State Legislatures, 2
Functions, 9
The State Legislature in a Changing Society, 21

II APPORTIONMENT AND ELECTIONS
page 24

Historical Background of the "Reapportionment Revolution," 24
Problems of Apportionment, 28
Results of Apportionment Systems, 31
Election Systems, 34
Conclusion, 37

III RECRUITMENT AND COMPOSITION
page 39

Party Competition, 39
Composition, 44
Tenure and Turnover, 48
Compensation, 50
Legislative Responsibility and Legislative Turnover, 52

vii

IV STRUCTURE AND PROCEDURE
page 55

Leadership, 57
Committees, 61
Staff Services, 67
Sessions, 77
Procedural Rules, 77
Group Norms, 83

V EXTERNAL FORCES
page 85

Constituency, 86
Party, 90
Interest Groups, 96
The Governor, 99
Conclusion, 102

VI THE FUTURE OF STATE LEGISLATURES
page 103

Reform Proposals, 105
Achieving Reform, 109

INDEX
page 115

STATE LEGISLATIVE SYSTEMS

1 INTRODUCTION

A legislature is an institution within which individuals deliberate, debate, and decide on matters of policy affecting the distribution of social values among those whom they represent. Making public law in this fashion might be called the characteristic function of a legislature in the American system. This activity, however, may be combined with a number of related activities such as: (1) checking the administrative branch of government; (2) educating the public about matters of general social and political importance; (3) conducting investigations; (4) impeaching executive officials; or even (5) selecting executive leaders.[1] These tasks will be performed in varying degrees and with varying measures of success, depending on the legal and political framework of the particular legislature; but whatever the particular "mix" of activities performed by the legislature, it is likely to be an important structure for "establishing and maintaining the legal order, crystallizing and settling conflict, determining priorities, granting

[1] For an expanded discussion of these various activities of legislature, both national and state, see the introductory chapter of William J. Keefe and Morris S. Ogul, *The American Legislative Process: Congress and the States* (Englewood Cliffs, N.J.: Prentice-Hall, Inc., 1964); and Malcolm E. Jewell and Samuel C. Patterson, *The Legislative Process in the United States* (New York: Random House, 1966), Chap. 1. Also of interest is George S. Blair's account of the American experience in *American Legislatures: Structure and Practice* (New York: Harper & Row, Publishers, 1967), chaps. 1,2.

1

legitimacy to policies, and adapting existing rules of society to new conditions."[2]

Each of the fifty American states has a legislature whose task, in theory, is to make laws for the state. But the manner in which this task is to be carried out is specified in only rudimentary fashion by the United States Constitution. In particular, the states are required to have a "republican," or representative, form of government. The actual configuration of institutions is left to the discretion of the states, and a strict parallel to the national pattern of separation of powers into executive, legislative, and judicial branches is not required. Each state has the power to adapt the national theme to its local political culture and institutions, but not one state has taken advantage of the opportunity to improvise on these fundamental principles, and only Nebraska has ceased to follow the national pattern of a two-house legislature. Because the states have not been innovators, their operation of the legislative process has developed similarly. Describing its common characteristics will be our chief objective; but we shall also comment on procedural differences among legislatures, political characteristics, and the general social environment that impinges on the legislative process.[3]

HISTORICAL TRENDS IN STATE LEGISLATURES

Foremost among the factors common to American state legislatures are the trends in their status, from the beginning of our independence to the present.[4]

Following the English model of a parliament, each of the Thirteen Colonies had a legislative body. Much of the controversy leading to the Revolution involved the conflict between these representative bodies and other appointed officials—notably the governors and other magistrates, who were often more responsive to the King of England than to their colonial constituency. Accordingly, when the representatives of the Colonies declared their independence in 1776, the prevailing pattern among the new states became one of legislative supremacy. Having struggled so long against what they regarded as oppressive executives, the Americans preferred to have most power vested in elected representative bodies.

The Articles of Confederation, which established the new nation in 1781, provided for a central legislative body and made virtually no allowance for an executive agency. Decisions made by the representa-

[2]Keefe and Ogul, *ibid.*, p. 1.

[3]Since the emphasis will be on general characteristics of legislatures, discussion of particular states will be fairly limited and presented only as examples. Students concerned with the specifics of an individual state may obtain information from subsequent tables reproduced from *The Book of States* and from selected bibliographic references in the footnotes.

[4]Portions of the following discussion draw heavily on Wilder W. Crane, Jr., "Legislators and the Formulation of Public Purpose," in John C. Wahlke and Alex N. Dragnich, eds., *Government and Politics: An Introduction to Political Science* (New York: Random House, 1966), pp. 460–89, in which there is a more general treatment of foreign governments.

tives (who were chosen as delegates of a *state*, not of a district) were binding only by mutual consent, and there was no provision for a coercive executive power that could enforce decisions. The new nation, then, was primarily a voluntary organization in which the primary units were states, and which did not have an agency that could reduce the sovereignty of the constituent units without their consent. Significantly, the Articles did not provide for the extraction of taxes from American citizens or for the raising of an army, except as the states felt constrained to acquiesce to such decisions in the central legislative body. On the state level, this fear of powerful executives was manifested in a somewhat similar fashion, and governors were generally accorded powers far inferior to those of the legislatures. The primary function of the governor, as conceived by the colonists, was to carry out policy that had been specified in the constituent assembly—not to initiate policy or exert a power independent of the legislature. Powers of innovation and decision-making were thereby lodged in a series of relatively powerful representative assemblies which, in turn, sent delegates to a "confederal" national assembly to make whatever minimal decisions were necessary to keep the new nation intact.

Even after 1789, when the Constitution superceded the Articles of Confederation and established a federal form of government, the legislatures were dominant in the individual states. The new prescription was for a separation of powers in which the executive, legislative, and judicial had certain powers independent of the others, while sharing the major functions of government. This, however, did not serve to reduce the legislative dominance in the states; in fact, it was so pronounced that the Founding Fathers of the national government were not certain that separation of powers could be realized at the national level. In *The Federalist* Madison expressed concern that the "parchment barriers" of a constitution would not restrain the "encroaching spirit of power" of the legislature, since, he argued, "the legislative department is everywhere extending the sphere of its activity and drawing all power into its impetuous vortex."[5]

On the state level, the nineteenth century saw a shift in the balance of power between the legislative and executive branches of government, and there was a progressive decline in the relative status of state legislatures. At the beginning of the century, governors began to develop powers independent of the legislature. This alteration in the configuration of power was not drastic but appeared to be an incremental process whereby governors (as an institution) came to be somewhat more trusted. The model of the President on the national level may have provided some assurance that an executive need not be dictatorial. Furthermore, the new nation was gaining experience in governing itself without the incubus of a colonial power, and its experiences tended to modify its former fears of the executive branch. The increased recognition of the value of an independent executive, however, did not mean automatic growth of the governors' power. The era

[5]Clinton Rossiter, ed., *The Federalist* (Chicago: The New American Library, 1961), pp. 308–9.

of Jacksonian Democracy provided checks on the executive that are still operative.

In the Jacksonian period — beginning approximately with the Presidency of Andrew Jackson in 1828 — several governmental improvisations were tried in an attempt to provide open access to public office and public decision-making by more members of society. Although it is perhaps not correct to call Jackson a "proletarian President," it is true that his administration brought an increased agrarian outlook to the national executive and opposed elitism (at least of New England merchants) in national office.[6] "King Caucus"—the practice of nominating American presidents in congressional caucus — gave way to the presidential nominating convention, and the method of electing executives on the state level was also subjected to revision. In particular, the so-called "plural executive" gained increased influence.

The plural executive is a product of multiple elections to the executive branch of the government; the secretary of state and other officers run independently of the governor, thereby loosening obligations between the governor and those whose cooperation he must have in running the government. The President selects his Secretary of State, Attorney General, and other members of the appointive entourage, but many governors were—and some still are—deprived of this critical power. Consequently, a governor may have a high-ranking executive—including his lieutenant governor—who is from the opposition. Even if the independently elected officials are in the governor's party, their individual success often makes them feel politically independent of the chief executive.[7]

Thus, the national trend for the augmentation of executive powers was in many states combined with a countertrend that tended to produce political in-fighting among the state's executive leadership. On the one hand, direct election of these officials deprived the legislature of supremacy over the executive; on the other, the multiplicity of power points in the executive branch often worked to deprive the governor of his influence over the legislative process.

The nadir of integrity in state legislatures came after the Civil War, when they were often blatantly corrupt and declined considerably in public esteem and power. In this era of industrial expansion and the burgeoning of American capitalism, corporate interests such as the railroad were of prodigious power in many state legislatures. The influence of special economic interests was further multiplied by the arrangement whereby senators were elected to the national Congress by the state legislatures. Until direct election of senators was instituted by constitutional amendment in 1913, inequities and corruption in state legislatures did much to tarnish the image of the United States Senate also.

Popular response to this corruption resulted in constitutional restrictions on the power of state legislatures. The wave of deficit spending of

[6]See Richard Hofstadter, *The American Political Tradition* (New York: Random House, 1948), pp. 45–67.

[7]The classic analysis of this characteristic of plural executives is in V. O. Key, Jr., *American State Politics* (New York: Alfred A. Knopf, Inc., 1956), pp. 197–216.

the 1820's and 1830's for "internal improvements"—generally subsidies for railroads, roads, and canals—led to defaults in state debts during the economic setback of 1837 and later.[8] Carpetbag governments in the South during Reconstruction issued bonds, but often reneged on the payments and subsequently paid only a portion of the scaled-down estimate of indebtedness.[9] Public reaction to these and other irresponsible actions of state governments led to constitutional provisions against deficit spending. In addition, legislatures were required to limit the length of their sessions (perhaps on the assumption that anything they would do would be bad). Characteristic prohibitions such as those terminating the power of legislatures to charter corporations or to grant divorces probably did not diminish legislative power; but other restrictions, notably on taxation and spending, seriously limited legislative discretion.

The increase in the power of the executive in the twentieth century brought about an even greater decline in the status of state legislatures. As states assumed more and more functions, the administration became increasingly larger. As the nature of government regulation became too complex to be dealt with by statutes, more and more vital decisions were made by executive order and administrative rule-making. As the administration grew in size, the need for more effective control by the governor increased; but these controls often decreased the power of the legislature. For example, nearly all states have instituted the executive budget, which enables the governor to develop a comprehensive fiscal program; but the executive budget transfers the initiative in spending and in taxation—the most important functions of government—from the legislature to the governor.

This brief discussion makes it clear that the status of the legislature compared to other agencies of governmental power has declined since the American Republic was established. Yet, as K. C. Wheare points out in his discussion of legislatures throughout the world, this decline is relative, not absolute.[10] Most state legislatures may deal with matters of great importance and spend enormous sums of money—far more so than in Colonial times or even in the nineteenth century; but other agencies of government, such as the executive and the judiciary, have grown even more in importance, so that the power of the legislature is relatively decreased. Furthermore, a distinction must be made between the notions of a *decline in power* and a *decline in efficiency*. The former refers to the relationship between the legislature and other structures of government; the latter refers to the manner in which the work of the assembly is expedited. In the second regard, state legislatures have improved considerably.

Legislative reference agencies, bill drafting services, legislative councils, and committee staffs have certainly made twentieth-century legislatures far more efficient than they were in the days of alleged

[8]See James A. Maxwell, *Financing State and Local Governments* (Washington, D.C.: The Brookings Institution, 1965), p. 180.

[9]*Ibid.*

[10]*Legislatures* (New York: Oxford University Press, 1963), pp. 219–34 (esp. p. 222).

legislative supremacy. Legislators themselves and many other persons are directing their efforts at increasing the efficiency of these representative institutions. (The last chapter of this volume will describe in greater detail the work of groups who are striving to improve legislatures.) Actual work and production of legislatures has greatly increased in recent years, and certainly the standard of ethics of mid-twentieth century American legislators is higher than it was during the corrupt era in the late nineteenth century.[11] It is therefore inaccurate to speak of a decline in the efficiency or ethics of legislatures. If state legislatures are declining in power, their decline, like that of legislatures throughout the world, is relative to the executive and not absolute.

The alleged decline in the status of state legislatures is like, and related to, the alleged decline in the power of the states in their relationships with the national government. Although the great increase in the power of the national government attracts most attention, the states are performing more services and employing more persons than ever before. Since World War II, the rate of increase in state spending has far exceeded the rate of increase in national government spending. To the extent that state legislatures make decisions concerning these increased functions of government, they have become more important than they were a century ago, when state functions were minimal.

State-level expenditures have indeed shown steady rises partly due to the increase in revenue and expenditures brought about by natural economic growth, and partly due to the inauguration of new policies aimed at the satisfaction of constituency demands. Even more important is the fact that state expenditures have grown at least as rapidly as federal expenditures. Thus, the amount of state participation in statewide functions has not shown any sign of decreasing; compared to federal expenditures, state activity has actually increased as a proportion of the total. One way of assessing this change is to compare the proportions of the gross national product that the various governmental levels are able to spend.

Figure 1 illustrates the extent to which federal and state-local sources have increased their demands on the gross national product of the United States since the turn of the century. Absolute expenditures will naturally tend to rise over the years because of the changing cost of items that governments must purchase, the increasing numbers of citizens for whom services must be provided, and any general inflationary tendencies that may exist in the economy. However, in addition to such "natural" increases in expenditures, there is a marked tendency for government in general to take a bigger slice of the nation's social product. With the increasing complexity of American society and the growing demands of its members for services, a greater proportion of

[11]This judgment about the decrease in corruption in state legislatures from the nineteenth century to the present should not obscure the fact that there are periodic revivals in the concern over corruption and inefficiencies in state legislatures. For two examples in popular magazines, see (State Senator) Paul Simon, "The Illinois Legislature: A Study in Corruption," *Harper's Magazine,* September, 1964 and Trevor Armbrister, "The Octopus in the State House," *The Saturday Evening Post,* February 12, 1966.

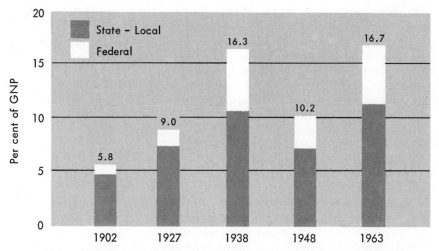

From James A. Maxwell, *Financing State and Local Government* (Washington, D. C.: The Brookings Institution, 1965), p. 22.

FIG. 1. General expenditure for civil functions by all levels of government as percentage of GNP, selected years, 1902 – 1963. (Intergovernmental payments are charged to the level of government making final disbursement.)

the gross national product is being allocated for government-directed civil functions. It can be seen from the chart that the governmental share of the national productivity reached a peak in around 1938, when most of the social legislation of the New Deal was in force and the nation was in the process of pulling itself out of a severe economic depression. Furthermore, the nation was not at that time engaged in any large-scale military operations that would tend to siphon off governmental funds into defense spending.

In the years following 1938, the United States became involved in a world war which greatly increased the proportion of the gross national product diverted for governmental purposes. Little of this increase, however, redounded to the benefit of the state and local governments. On the contrary, state and local expenditures declined as a proportion of the gross national product, while federal expenditures increased. Domestic policies (here classified as "civil functions") were often deferred as the war effort took an increasing bite out of the available tax resources, manpower, and consumable materials. Since the end of World War II, however, civil expenditures have shown a marked tendency to rise in proportion to the GNP, and one can see in Fig. 1 that by 1963 the total governmental demand on the social product was back up to its 1938 level.

The most important characteristic of these data is the relative weighting of federal, as opposed to state and local, expenditures. Contrary to the charge that the federal government is expanding to the detriment of inferior levels of government stands the more accurate assertion that all levels of government are expanding their respective powers and functions. Although it may be true that the federal government has increased its total expenditures (including defense) more rapidly than have state governments, it should also be recognized that state and local agencies still spend the most money on civil and peacetime functions.[12] It is they who make some of the most important decisions about the proper allocation of expenditures, and it is they who must bear much of the burden of finding appropriate tax sources for raising funds. The state government, with its primary responsibility for such costly programs as public education, highways, and welfare, exists as an important source of public policies that affect nearly all citizens.

Furthermore, state legislators spend more time at legislative tasks, as one state after another moves from biennial to annual—and longer—sessions. They have enlarged budgets and raised taxes in almost every state, each session, during the past thirty years; and every state continues to pile up statutes as society, becoming more urban and industrial, adds to the complexity of regulation and services required.

In general, the urbanization and industrialization in the first half of the twentieth century have produced a society increasingly more complex in each succeeding decade of its existence. This complexity is itself an important consequence. It is transmitted into the political system in the form of competing, cross-cutting allegiances that may be characterized in terms of well-known, but sometimes vague, social and economic categories; e.g., ethnicity, socio-economic status, regionalism, historical loyalty, religious affiliation, and relation to the major productive processes of society. The composite picture that arises is one of diversity—a diversity that produces more or less "natural" disharmonies among various interests. These disharmonies in the social system strain the legislature's (and usually the individual legislator's) ability to decide upon an acceptable allocation of the social product among competing interests, and these tensions tend to multiply the number of demands to which the legislature must react. The law-making body will therefore have to make more decisions than before, and the consequences of these decisions will be more intricate and often difficult to predict. Thus whereas the injection of social wants increases the need for governmental success, the number of chances for failure (either of commission or omission) also increases at a rapid pace. At the same time, if the political system is to maintain its position as a goal-setting, order-maintaining institution, it must become more responsive as society's demands become more numerous. Thus although we may speak of the decline of the legislature relative to the executive, we are

[12]For readable and informative treatments of these topics, the reader might consult James A. Maxwell, *op. cit.,* especially Chap. I and Frederick C. Mosher and Orville F. Poland, *The Costs of American Governments* (New York: Dodd, Mead & Co., 1964), especially Chap. 3. An older but quite useful treatment of government economics is Solomon Fabricant's *The Trend of Government Activity in the United States Since 1900* (New York: National Bureau of Economic Research, Inc., 1952). For a more policy-oriented treatment of governmental welfare functions, Wayne Vasey's *Governmental and Social Welfare* (New York: Holt, Rinehart & Winston, Inc., 1958) is useful.

still dealing with a vital institution—an institution within which many of the dominant trends in social and economic change in the United States come to a focal point.

FUNCTIONS

The first page of this volume stated that legislatures *in theory* make the laws for the state. The classic doctrine of Montesquieu—that legislatures make the law, courts interpret the law, and executives carry out the law—was never a valid description of any government, and it certainly fails to describe adequately the function of American state legislatures. Legislatures are not the exclusive lawmaking authority in the states; nor are they lawmakers exclusively.

The legislature shares its lawmaking authority with many other institutions and groups.

The governor and other executives play an important role in lawmaking.[13] The governor assumes the initiative in proposing legislation. Citizens expect him to have a legislative program, and they are impressed more by his ability to put it through than by his administrative activities, of which they have only a vague notion. It is, in fact, increasingly common to refer to the governor as chief legislator. Paralleling the powers of the President on the national level, most governors are empowered to give a "state of the state" address in which they outline their major policy goals for the legislature, and like the President, governors often make use of their "message power" to deliver special communications to the legislature. Naturally the governor is not permitted to introduce legislation personally in the assembly; however, the formal introduction of a bill is normally made in the name of a sympathetic legislator, and there is seldom much doubt about its actual source. A key indicator of this relationship between the chief executive and the legislature is often the name used in sponsorship: in many legislatures the official sponsor is the floor leader of the governor's party.

Furthermore, the governor may send aides to speak on behalf of his proposals before legislative committees or may even personally attempt to persuade legislators to support his proposals. By means of these and similar tactics, the governor can act not only as the chief initiator of legislation, but also as the chief lobbyist for major policy proposals.

In addition, the governor commands a platform of public visibility and moral suasion that cannot be matched by legislators, since his "constituency" is the whole electorate of the state. Appeals for support through the mass media are more likely to have an effect when they emanate from the single podium of the Executive Office than from the many smaller voices in the representative assembly.

[13]See Chap. V for a more detailed discussion of the governor's role as chief legislator.

The governor's position as the formal head of his party also gives him political powers that can rarely be matched by others. This symbolic position is all the more enhanced when the governor is personally persuasive or has substantial patronage power, which can make him more capable of eliciting support among his party's legislative delegation.

Calling special sessions for the purpose of considering legislation is another positive power of the governor. In many cases, the business conducted in a special session can deal only with the particular subject specified by the chief executive. This power allows the governor to reconvene legislatures that may have shunted off to the end of the session bills he considered important for legislative action. When the constitution provides that no new bills be introduced during the special session and that only a limited range of policy (that specified by the executive) may be considered, this power is all the greater.

On the negative side, the governor influences legislation by his use of threat of *veto*. A general veto constitutes a gubernatorial rejection of the entire bill; however, some governors are further empowered to use an *item veto*, which can be used to reject only objectionable segments of the proposal while allowing the rest to become law.[14] An item veto is particularly useful in blocking amendments or riders that may be added by the legislature to a bill that the governor favors. Where the item veto is not allowed, the legislature can often force a governor to accept a few passages that he might otherwise oppose; in this way, the representative can capitalize on the governor's reluctance to "throw out the baby with the bathwater."

The governor is not the only executive who may initiate legislative proposals. Other officials, in the process of administering programs, see the need for new legislation and find means to have proposals introduced and enacted by the legislature.

After laws have been enacted, the administration of them involves subsidiary forms of lawmaking. As society and technology become more complex, it is no longer possible to spell out all possible details in statutes. Thus, considerable rule-making authority must be delegated to administrators, especially state regulatory agencies. The specific rules made by these agencies may be more important than the general statutes enacted by the legislature. In the extreme case, this practice of administrative rule-making may correspond roughly to the British practice of "delegated" legislation—a procedure whereby skeleton laws are filled in by the executive branch in charge of administering the law. Although such "delegated" legislation is normally contrary to American practice (at least in a constitutional sense), various aspects of administrative rule-making often surpass the wishes of the legislature.

[14]For more on gubernatorial veto powers, see F. W. Prescott, "The Executive Veto in the American States," *Western Political Quarterly*, III (1950), 98–112. A useful tabulation of gubernatorial veto powers appears in Joseph A. Schlesinger, "The Politics of the Executive," in Herbert Jacob and Kenneth N. Vines, eds., *Politics in the American States: A Comparative Analysis* (Boston: Little, Brown & Co., 1965), p. 227. Table 5–2 of this volume includes a summary chart of gubernatorial powers derived from Schlesinger's discussion.

Courts make laws.   In all American states except Louisiana,[15] common law, which is entirely judge-made law, is applied to cases not covered by the statutes. Moreover, all American state courts have the right of judicial review and thus may find statutes enacted by the legislature unconstitutional. And in the very process of interpreting law, courts may be making law, for the legislative intent is often not clear.

Citizens make laws.   The era of Jacksonian democracy left many of the American states with the practices of *initiative* and *referendum*, whereby citizens can participate directly in the lawmaking process. Twenty states allow for the initiative by which, if a certain percentage of voters sign a petition, a proposed law must be considered. Sixteen states have the direct initiative, under which a proposal must be directly submitted to the people at an election rather than sent to the legislature. The reasoning behind this provision apparently was that initiative would not be used by the public unless a legislature was unresponsive; therefore the bill proposed by the people should not have to run the risk of sabotage by the same truculent assembly. When the public has the opportunity to vote on a bill, the result is a rare instance of "direct democracy"—a referendum in which the people directly vote on public policy rather than express their preferences through elected representatives. Twenty-nine states have some form of this referendum procedure.

Lawmaking at the state level is also delegated, in effect, to select groups of citizens in occupational associations—medical, legal, real-estate, for example—who are empowered to set standards and control participation in their own activities. Medical associations, state bar associations, cosmeticians, and even some organized skill groups in unions receive from the state government the privilege of determining who is qualified to practice that profession, trade, or craft. From a governmental point of view, this places the function of specifying certain public standards in the hands of specialized private groups.

Turning now from the agencies that share with legislatures the task of making public laws and regulations, we must note certain functions performed by legislatures that are not, strictly speaking, legislative. To be sure, much of the work of a legislature exceeds the specification of public goals through statutory law. Lawmaking as a governmental power is augmented in most state legislatures by administrative, judicial, and other activities as discussed below.

Administrative

Among the various ways of participating in administrative activities, making appropriations for them places the legislature in the best position for keeping an eye on administrative agencies. Legislators are

[15]Louisiana law derives much of its legal structure from the Continental custom of "codified law" and thus reflects its heritage as part of the French colonial empire. The remainder of the United States draws its legal tradition from the Anglo-Saxon custom of "common law," according to which judicial decisions enter the corpus of law and serve as precedents for deciding future cases.

rarely cited for their vigilance and effective use of this vantage point; but knowing that the legislators are there, administrators are influenced by the fact that the hand that opens the wallet is related to a voice that can question minor details. On the national level, the Truman investigations into World War II spending (Truman was then a U.S. senator), the McCarthy investigations into State Department activities, and the annual congressional hearings on the budget offer diverse examples of legislative involvement in the process of administration and administrative policy-making. Although the public impact of legislative oversight on the state level is seldom so substantial, the principle remains the same.

The biggest limitation on the use of the power of administrative surveillance is in the *quality of information* that the legislature is able to command. In nearly every case, the administrative official who is to be examined will be superior in the amount and quality of information that he possesses. If the legislators choose to be cowed by his expertise and concede their political prerogatives to the specialist, there is little hope that the intervention of the legislature in the process of administration will be effective (whether for good or for ill).[16] In short, there is an element of tension between the administrative agencies and the legislature by the very nature of their differential tasks. They must cooperate to some degree, but each has different power resources to draw upon in the event of conflict. The bureaucracy has an arcanum of regulations that will remain somewhat mystifying to the legislature, and it can draw upon superior information. The legislature can speak symbolically with the voice of the people: it can withhold funds, and with luck, it can develop a measure of technical expertise. But a state legislature — with its short terms, rapid turnover of personnel, and relatively modest incentives for excellence — is generally not on its best footing when trying to engage in administrative functions in this fashion.

Legislators also spend a great deal of time in specific administrative matters when they undertake errand-running for their constituents. Operating without the staffs that congressmen have for casework, they spend countless hours getting in touch with state agencies on behalf of their constituents. An example of this relationship between the legislator and the agencies of state administration was expressed by a state representative this way:

A good legislator in my opinion should be willing to serve as a contact between his constituents and the various departments of state government; in other words, he should be a sort of walking directory so that he can at least refer his citizens to the right person or department when they have a problem at the state level. That I feel is a part of the service he should be willing to render when he takes the oath of office.[17]

[16]For a recent discussion of this problem on the national level, see Lewis A. Dexter, "'Check and Balance' Today: What Does It Mean for Congress and Congressmen?" in *Congress: The First Branch of Government* (Washington, D.C.: The American Enterprise Institute for Public Policy Research, 1966), pp. 83–113.

[17]John C. Wahlke, Heinz Eulau, William Buchanan, and LeRoy C. Ferguson, *The Legislative System: Explorations in Legislative Behavior* (New York: John Wiley & Sons, Inc., 1962), p. 306.

His relations with constituents in his own district make it necessary for a legislator to gain at least some knowledge of the administrative apparatus in his state, perhaps even to the extent of becoming a "walking directory." In addition, many of the "errand boy" tasks that he performs will be administrative and not legislative in nature.

Constituent

Legislators perform constituent functions when they participate in constitution-making. On the national level, legislators can propose amendments to the United States Constitution if two-thirds of the state legislatures meet and agree to the suggested alterations.[18] Ratification of amendments in the United States is normally performed by state legislatures (three-fourths of all the legislatures must ratify). On the state level, these functions include arranging constitutional conventions, voting on—and submitting—proposed constitutional amendments to the electorate, and enacting statutes to fill gaps in the constitution.

Judicial

Legislators perform judicial functions when they consider impeachments of state officials. Confirming judicial appointments is a common function of legislatures and is usually done by the senate. The establishment of courts, the determination of judges' salaries, and the determination of the jurisdiction of courts are not, strictly speaking, judicial functions. But these activities of the state legislature do give it some access to the administration of justice in the state and involve it in the judicial process. Thus, the state legislature performs in a *judicial capacity* when it considers impeachments, and it engages in the wider *judicial process of the state* when it considers appointments and legislates in the area of judicial practice.

Electoral

Some state legislatures perform electoral functions. A significant, if somewhat atypical, example is that of Tennessee, where the governor is the only official who is elected on the statewide ballot; other state officers are elected by the legislature. On the surface, this structural feature of Tennessee government would seem to place a sturdy weapon in the hands of the state legislators since they might, at will, burden the governor with executive officers (secretary of state, for example) whose allegiance would be to a legislative clique and not to their chief executive. It might even provide closer legislative rapport with the lower executive officers than with the governor, thereby decreasing the chief executive's legislative initiative and severely restricting his freedom of action. In short, one might expect this procedure to pit the legislature and chief executive against one another on many crucial matters. But the result has been different

---

[18] Although this means has not been successful in the past, there was a flurry of state legislative activity in 1967 to propose a variation on the "Dirksen amendment," which sought to provide a constitutional basis for apportionment on some basis other than population. It was an attempt to "overrule" the Supreme Court on the question of apportionment.

In Tennessee, the governor takes an active part in designating the *leadership in the legislature:* the Speakers in both houses are generally nominated by party caucuses (usually Democratic) and must be acceptable to the governor. Furthermore, as Wahlke and his associates report, there are "administration floor leaders" in both houses; presumably this is an alternative designation to "majority party leader" and reflects the executive's control over legislative leadership selection.[19] Thus, the Tennessee variant of leadership selection—both to the legislative and executive branches—does not reflect the conflict that one might expect from its structural arrangements. The intervening factors of *party discipline* and *gubernatorial influence* seem to be the most important aspects of the process.

Another electoral function, often overlooked because of its infrequent application, is the legislature's role in electing a member of the executive branch when the public mandate is unclear: when neither candidate receives a majority of the votes cast for that office. On the state level, there is no electoral college to resolve an occasional election in which there is no clear majority (as in the Truman election of 1948 and the Kennedy election of 1960). For the Presidency, when no candidate receives a majority in the electorate, the distribution of electoral college votes usually resolves possible conflict by creating the semblance of a majority. On the state level, however, an inconclusive balloting is resolved by the legislature—a tactic invoked nationally only when the electoral college is deadlocked (and this has never happened).[20]

A recent use of this electoral function by a legislature can be seen in the election of Lester Maddox as Governor of Georgia. Maddox was challenged by "Bo" Calloway to an inconclusive duel for the governorship in 1966. Lacking a majority, both candidates had the alternative of leaving the decision to the Georgia legislature. In spite of Calloway's dilatory attempts to obtain a new public ballot, or some other electoral device that might better his chance of election, Maddox, the Democrat, was chosen governor by the Democratic Georgia legislature. Although such events are rare in the American states, their occurrence serves at times to give a bonus to the party in control of the legislature and to allow the legislators to pick their governor.

Investigatory

Like the national Congress, state legislatures have the right to investigate and the power to subpoena witnesses. These legislative privileges should be distinguished from the right of the legislature to oversee administrative agencies. In many areas the functions overlap; however, administrative oversight can be considered an ongoing enterprise and

[19] Wahlke *et al., The Legislative System: Explorations in Legislative Behavior,* pp. 56–59.

[20] The closest the United States came to electing a President in the House of Representatives was in 1876, when two delegations from Mississippi tried to gain official recognition in the electoral college. One delegation was for Hayes; the other favored Tilden. The outcome of the electoral college vote depended on which group was recognized; however, rather than throw the balloting into the House, a compromise was worked out in a congressional committee that accepted the Hayes delegation and granted other concessions to Tilden supporters.

part of the normal *modus operandi* of the representative body's business. Quite often, hearings are carried out by a committee or subcommittee that is designated as the watchdog for a particular branch of the executive or a committee that considers itself responsible for a particular aspect of policy (e.g., budget, labor, education, commerce, and highway committees).

Investigations are normally instituted when an offense—perhaps illegal conduct—is suspected. The subpoena becomes crucial to the conduct of an investigation when witnesses may be unwilling to disclose information about their activities because of the quasi-judicial nature of the proceedings. (At regular committee hearings, witnesses are often anxious to appear, in order to present their case for a particular bill or to make their policy position known to the legislature.) Counterpart to these investigations on the national level might be the Kefauver investigations of organized crime and the McClellan-Kennedy investigations of alleged labor racketeering. Naturally, such activities in the states are on a smaller scale and are publicized to a lesser extent, but the power to investigate does exist and can be invoked to study alleged problems and abuses and to obtain information that might facilitate the drafting of corrective legislation. Despite these justifications, we should not forget that investigations can also be used to aggrandize the personal career of an ambitious legislator, undermine an executive whom the investigating committee may not favor, and embarrass people whom crusading legislators might not otherwise be able to single out (as in the case of loyalty-security investigations).

Lawmaking

Having considered the lawmaking functions of nonlegislators and the nonlawmaking functions of legislators, we now may discuss what is, in theory, the primary function of state legislatures. The legislature does in fact make the laws of the state, for the approval of citizens' representatives gives legitimacy to the coercive norms of the society. Thus, although a decision may actually have been made elsewhere and simply brought to the legislature for ratification, it is the approval by the legislature that makes the decision authoritive in the minds of the governed.

At its weakest, then, the state legislature is a legitimating body through which programs must pass before they become law. Where the legislature is impotent or has surrendered its prerogatives, it may do little more than ratify proposals conceived in the office of the governor. A picture somewhat more congenial, at least to the traditions of American prescriptive political science, is one in which the legislature is a "broker" of diverse interests—an institution that embraces the body politic and provides a forum for the representation of the voters' needs and for the deliberation of public policy. It is also possible to view the state legislature as an experimental testing ground for new ideas and new legislation that might eventually be taken up by other governments after a suitable period of examination. For example, the Wisconsin income tax and unemployment compensation preceded the current

federal laws, and Oklahoma experimented with bank deposit guarantees before the federal government accepted the program.[21] But whatever description fits a particular legislature—passive ratifier, broker of
interests, bold innovator—constitutional provision and public expecta-
tion give it the central task of promulgating public law. Performing this
function as the agent of the people, the representative body also con-
fers legitimacy on the acts of government. The particular image that
applies to an individual institution (innovator, ratifier, broker) depends
largely on the verve and perspicacity with which the legislature carries
out this basic task.

A bill that has been approved by a legislature—in other words, a
product of the legislature—is called a statute. In the hierarchy of laws,
a statute ranks below the constitution but takes precedence over other
laws such as common law, executive orders, or municipal ordinances.
Common law, as made by judges, is applied only in the absence of a
statute, and at any time the state legislature may specifically modify or
abolish common-law provisions. Executive orders and administrative
regulations may be issued only pursuant to statutes. Accordingly, when
the legislature does not approve of decisions made by these agencies, it
may amend the statutes to impose its own guidelines for decisions.

All enactments of local units of government are subordinate to the
enactments of the state legislature, but unlike the relationships between
the national government and the states in the American federal system,
local units of government within the states are regarded as agencies of
the states and thus possess no rights adverse to the state. In spite of the
fact that counties often have a tenacious political existence that is
worthy of respect by the state legislature, their legal status is that of
administrative units in most areas. In most states, cities are wholly dependent on the state legislature, since it has prior and exclusive rights
over most tax sources and has the greatest potential fiscal ability. Often
property taxes accrue to local levels of government to finance local
policies, and cities like Chicago are allowed to add a fraction of a cent to
the sales tax; these fiscal sources, however, exist largely at the pleasure
of the state legislature (as frustrated Chicago officials will not hesitate to
explain). Legally, the state legislatures maintain even the right to create
or abolish local units of government and establish their jurisdiction at
will, although the political ramifications of such action tend to stay the
hand of the legislature.

Following the "Dillon's Rule" dictum of 1872 (named for the Iowa
judge who first enunciated the principle), any doubt in resolving a
conflict between the state and its subdivisions is to be decided in favor
of the state. Some state legislatures have indeed granted municipalities
certain rights called "home rule," but such rights are subject to amendment by the state legislature. Even in circumstances in which a broad
general power has been delegated to municipalities, the state legislature
may enact statutes dealing with the specifics within the general field.
For example, although the statutes may assign a broad power over fire

[21] See Maxwell, *Financing State and Local Governments*, pp. 29–30.

departments to cities, the state legislature may decide to regulate the wages or hours of the firemen.[22]

Unlike Congress, which is specifically authorized by the Constitution to legislate only in certain fields, state legislatures have the power to act in any area, as long as their legislation is not counter to either national or state constitution. When one considers a proposal for national legislation, he must first determine whether Congress has the power to legislate in that field. On the state level, one needs to consider instead whether or not a proposal is inconsistent with the national or state constitutions; if it is not, the proposal may be enacted into law.

Once enacted, a national statute may be subject to review by United States courts; a state statute may be subject to review by the state supreme court, the United States Supreme Court, or perhaps even in one of the inferior courts in the federal system. In addition, a state law may come into conflict with the laws of another state (regulations of riparian rights might be an instance if two states disagree over uses of water) and as such would also be subject to review by the United States Supreme Court.

In essence, then, the critical questions on the authority of state legislatures are based on the restrictions in the national and state constitutions. One can read the national government's restrictions on the states in Article I, Section 10 of the original Constitution; they include the prohibitions against making treaties, engaging in war, coining money, passing bills of attainder or ex post facto laws, granting titles of nobility, and impairing the obligations of contracts. More important, however, are restrictions in the Fourteenth Amendment prohibiting the states from abridging the privileges and immunities of citizens, from denying persons the equal protection of the laws, and from depriving persons of life, liberty, or property without due process of law. These Fourteenth Amendment restrictions on the states have become increasingly important as the United States Supreme Court has expanded its definitions of what these phrases mean.

The original Constitution's Bill of Rights included, among other guarantees of personal freedom from persecution, a strict caveat to the national government that it should not abridge freedom of speech, assembly, or religion. The caveats, however, were not meant to apply to the state governments; they were accepted as amendments to the Constitution to assure citizens that the newly created national level of government would not become tyrannical. It was assumed that the state governments would make similar restrictions in their own constitutions or at least that citizens had less to fear because of the proximity of the state governments, and so no attempt was made to give the national

[22] For further information on "home rule," see G. Theodore Mitau, *State and Local Government: Politics and Processes* (New York: Charles Scribner's Sons, 1966), pp. 407–10; and Lyle E. Schaller, "Home Rule—A Critical Appraisal," *Political Science Quarterly,* LXXVI (January, 1961), 402–15. Additional references concerned with state-local relations are: Allen D. Manvel, "The States' Concern," *National Civic Review,* LI (February, 1962), 70–74; William I. Goodman, "Urban Planning and the Role of the State," *State Government,* XXXV (Summer, 1962), 149–54; and an older work, *The States and the Metropolitan Problem* (Chicago: The Council of State Governments, 1956).

level power to protect citizens from encroachments by the states. When a state did not provide immunities from persecution because of unpopular speech, for example, the national government was not empowered to intervene between the citizen and his state.

A landmark case in the redefinition of these First Amendment freedoms was *Gitlow* v. *New York* in 1925. Benjamin Gitlow, a leader of the American Communist party, was indicted by the state of New York for radical pamphleteering and similar activities that the state considered subversive. The case eventually reached the United States Supreme Court, where it was to be decided whether New York was actually abridging Gitlow's rights to freedom of speech. The Court's findings did not aid Gitlow very much, for his conviction was upheld. The Court ruled, however, that even though New York did not, in that instance, encroach on the citizen's rights, the United States Supreme Court could reserve the prerogative of review over such cases. In short, the outcome of the Gitlow case was not altered, but the national government was recognized by the high court as having the authority to protect citizens from persecution by state governments. As John Roche puts it,

...the Justices suggested that the due process clause of the Fourteenth Amendment established the same restrictions on the states that the First Amendment did on the federal government, that is, the substantive rights of speech, press, and opinion were protected from state invasion to the same extent that the national government was inhibited by the First Amendment...the principle was established: the Justices would exercise oversight of the activities of the state in limiting First Amendment Freedoms.[23]

It should be noted, however that some *procedural* guarantees are not included in recent Court decisions; rather, those of the First Amendment are considered to have a "preferred position" in the realm of civil liberties. Certain others—the Fifth Amendment provision against "double jeopardy," for example—historically have had diverse application from one state to another.

In recent years, the Fourteenth Amendment has assumed an even greater role in national-state relations. Especially since Earl Warren became Chief Justice, the rulings of the Court have had an increased impact on the states. The Court's definition of equal protection has been expanded to prohibit state-supported segregation in the schools and other public facilities. And the Court's interpretation of equal protection has been expanded since 1962 (*Baker* v. *Carr*) to require fundamental reapportionment of state legislatures. Congress has followed the Supreme Court's lead by passing a series of civil rights acts which, particularly in the field of voting rights, have further restricted the discretion of state legislatures.

But no matter how significant these national restrictions on the state legislatures might be, they are less important than the restrictions

[23]*Courts and Rights*, 2nd ed. (New York: Random House, 1966), pp. 78–79.

imposed within the states by their own state constitutions. No state legislature really wants to grant a title of nobility or coin money. The majority of states, even before the 1960's, did not have state requirements of segregation, nor did many of them deny persons the right to vote on account of race. In the 1890's, many states outside the South (e.g., Illinois, Wisconsin, Michigan) actually had civil rights legislation that was stronger than the national legislation in the 1960's. Thus the segregation decisions had a more selective effect than did the reapportionment cases, which had profound consequences for nearly all states in the Union.

In many ways, the constitutions of the states themselves are more of a burden to lawmaking than are the restrictions on the national level. And many of these restrictions derive from an era (generally from the middle to the late nineteenth century) when legislators were at a low point in popular esteem. It is not surprising to find that constitutions adopted in this period are far more restrictive than those adopted earlier. One of the most obvious means of preventing a legislature from doing very much was to restrict the length of legislative sessions. Thirty-three states still have such restrictions, some of which allow for as little as sixty days a year. Other restrictive provisions set forth many fields in which the legislature could not legislate. Limiting the state debt is one regulation that seems particularly debilitating to state legislatures, in light of the demands on government in the mid-twentieth century.

Although the national government may engage in deficit spending to finance projects that could not be undertaken on a "pay-as-you-go" basis, state governments often do not have this power. Although it varies from one state to another, many have a restriction that reflects popular reaction to fiscal irresponsibility in the 1830's and again after the Civil War. When debts were defaulted and legislators seemed not quite reliable with public funds, many constitutions specified that borrowing could not exceed a fixed amount. The maximum allowable in the state of Wisconsin, $100,000, perhaps seemed large when it was included in the constitution a century ago; however, that amount is quite small compared to annual budgets of more than a billion dollars in the 1960's. This artificial upper limit of spending capacity often works to keep the states from undertaking projects that the national government now carries out.

Large-scale public planning takes enormous amounts of money. Without substantial national participation, the states are not fiscally up to the task of supporting, say, urban renewal, highway construction, small-business loans, and area redevelopment (for encouraging industry and use of natural resources in underdeveloped areas). Thus the sword cuts in a manner unforeseen by the framers of state constitutions: it tends to limit the vitality of the whole state government and to shift a whole set of public demands for public programs to the national level. The result is often a weakening of the prerogatives of state government, and it leaves some legislatures open to the charge that they are simply "not able to cope with the twentieth century."

However, we should not slight the state legislatures on this score. As in other matters—both for good and for all—state legislatures have found means to circumvent strict interpretation of their limitations, so have they found ways to spend more money than is constitutionally allowed. Not all states with constitutional limits on spending find alternative mechanisms for obtaining funds, but some do. One such alternative mechanism is the "dummy corporation," as it is called in Wisconsin. Instead of declaring public indebtedness in the name of the state, a corporation consisting of the governor and selected legislative leaders borrows money for public projects. There is no doubt on the part of the lenders that the money is being used by the state government; the ruse of the "dummy corporation," however, avoids the constitutional stipulation preventing deficit spending.

Some restrictions on state legislatures derive from a bygone era when special interest groups succeeded in having essentially statutory provisions written into the constitution, although they have little place there. In order to protect its interests against any subsequent majority that might develop, a group that is dominant at the time may make substantial additions to the constitution—additions that are much more difficult to alter than simple statutes would be. In this way, the dead hand of an economic interest may be imposed on subsequent generations until an overwhelming majority can be rallied to amend the constitution. It is not unusual to find a constitutional amendment that governs the operation of grain elevators or the sale of livestock. Louisiana's constitution of 227,000 words, the longest of any state constitution, contains so many specific details—extending even to the particulars of garbage collection—that the legislature is strait-jacketed on almost any important issue it wants to consider. This situation suggests that rather than the traditional statute-making function, a more important operation of the Louisiana legislature has been to devise the 607 amendments (of which 460 were approved in referendum) submitted since the constitution was adopted in 1921.[24] (By way of contrast, recall that the national Constitution had 25 amendments in 1967, only 15 of which were passed after 1791.)

The practice of including special interests in the constitution is not necessarily a thing of the past. The legislatures of Arizona, Arkansas, Florida, Kansas, Mississippi, Nebraska, and South Dakota were willing to write in a "right to work" provision that was desired by businessmen. On the other side, the rights of workers to organize in labor unions and engage in collective bargaining was set down in the constitutions of Hawaii, Missouri, New Jersey, and New York.[25] Regardless of the substantive position one takes on any of these matters, it is clear that legislatures of today still labor under restrictions that were written into constitutional documents to ensure the advantage of particular groups;

[24] A more detailed, if somewhat dated, discussion of this problem is found in Kimbrough Owen, "The Need for Constitutional Revision in Louisiana," *Louisiana Law Review* (November, 1947). A useful general discussion of state constitutions with several tabular presentations can be found in G. Theodore Mitau, *op. cit.*, pp. 9–47.

[25] Mitau, *State and Local Government*, p. 13.

it is also clear that some legislatures are acting in turnabout fashion by imposing a similar dead hand on future legislatures. In this sense, state legislatures are often far more severely limited by their own constitutions than by the national Constitution.

THE STATE LEGISLATURE
IN A CHANGING SOCIETY

Much of the discussion to this point has stressed the nature of the challenge confronting most state legislatures in the mid-twentieth century. Several of the most important phenomena to which a legislature must respond are: 1) demographic change (shifts in the nature and location of the population); 2) industrial development; 3) urbanization; and 4) the differential distribution of affluence in society. Although this set of factors does not exhaust the potential list of challenges to a legislature's capabilities, it does include the developments that are most important to the emerging place of state government in the federal system. Linked to them are the questions of malapportionment, taxation, provision of major public services such as highways and education, and the extent of state participation in improving the welfare of its citizens. Whatever else a state legislature may do, it must eventually take some position regarding these questions. The manner in which the legislature adapts the structure of public policy to changing conditions becomes a matter of central importance, although the actual role it plays may vary considerably.

On the one hand, a political institution such as a legislature can take upon itself the task of setting the pace for development and change. On the state level, a governor or legislature can adopt policies to influence the pattern of future industrial settlement and can affect demographic movements. For example, a liberal package of old-age benefits may attract citizens of retirement age, progressive racial programs may attract minority groups from less liberal areas, and a healthy industrial climate may attract people into the state and from the farm to the city. State legislators and others often argue that a state's taxation policy has an influence on the location of industry; certainly the quality of its roads and the location of its labor force are important factors. Permissive incorporation laws may attract some types of corporate business into the state. The quality of its educational services will have an important effect on the life chances of the state's young people and may have an indirect affect on what John Stuart Mill called the "quality" of the citizenry. Furthermore, the generosity of its welfare programs may have important consequences for the less fortunate of its citizens. In all these examples, the political leadership in a state can directly or indirectly influence the course that social and economic change takes by using their positions to affect the distribution of social values.

On the other hand, the state legislature is subject to changes it cannot control, and in the reciprocal relationship between environmental and political change, it may be a follower rather than a leader. In an area undergoing social and economic change, new groups may arise on the basis of ethnic identification, status differential, occupational affiliation, or another basis of social cleavage. As these groups emerge and enter into the political system, they begin to make active demands on the rest of society. Often, of course, the demands of one group will be in disharmony with those of other groups, and the processing of conflicting demands may become an increasingly burdensome task for government. State legislators, among others, find that the industrialization and urbanization of their constituencies produce new clusters of individuals who bring different expectations into their political life as they vie for their "proper" shares of the social product. When these groups orient themselves to the political system as a source of policy to satisfy their wants, a burden is placed on its capacity to respond. This "politicization of wants," as David Easton calls it, can take many forms. A classic example is the ability of business and labor groups to alter the states' constitutions to include restriction or promotion of the right to organize and engage in collective bargaining (discussed above).[26] Often, when groups are unsuccessful in obtaining a legislative response that pleases them, they may shift their demands to another level of government. This tendency constitutes one of the major problems of state legislatures in America.

Because of alleged unresponsiveness of many state governments to problems of, say, urbanization and metropolitanization, demands from urban areas are being increasingly directed to other levels of government. New channels of influence may be sought, and the national government seems to be the major recipient of such demands. For example, urban areas have long complained that state legislatures did not adequately provide for their needs; as a result, most urban areas have found it possible to bypass the state government and establish direct communications with the federal government. A mayor of Chicago or New York will usually find a sympathetic ear in Washington, especially since American presidents are highly sensitive to the blocs of voters congregated in urban areas. If both the mayor and the President happen to be of the same party, the link between the city and Washington is even closer.

Notice also that such diverse programs as farm price supports and urban renewal both receive attention in Congress, since states generally cannot or will not embark on policies demanding such large cash outlays. Furthermore, specific interest groups in a state may object to paying taxes that do not directly aid them (farmers may not want to support urban welfare, city dwellers may oppose agricultural benefits), and, as a result, such major groups may band together with their counterparts in other states to request nationwide programs.

In essence, this upward shift of demands from the state to the national level of government is a consequence of the increasingly national

[26] See David Easton, *A Systems Analysis of Political Life* (New York: John Wiley & Sons, Inc., 1965), p. 80. William C. Mitchell uses similar imagery in *The American Polity* (New York: The Free Press, 1962), pp. 279–81.

focus of politics and social life in America. And this trend constitutes a constant challenge to each state's role as an important source of meaningful political action. Recognition of these problems prompted the late V. O. Key, Jr., to surmise that the states might well become "vestigial remnants left by the process of unification of separate entities into nationhood."[27]

On the more positive side, state government must be given its due (as we have argued above, with respect to increasing state expenditure levels). The states do, after all, have a vital hand in the distribution of important human values in society—to a large extent, they decide who gets what from government, and who pays the bill (by means of state taxation and expenditures). Large proportions of the total state budget are likely to be allocated for various forms of public welfare, education, and public safety. Highways and roads consume additional amounts of state revenues. States have primary responsibility for deciding internal political boundaries such as congressional districts, and they largely determine what requirements must be met by potential voters in order to receive the electoral franchise. Even where the federal government provides guidelines for state action through grants-in-aid and national legislation, the states largely determine the extent of their participation, the means of providing the necessary tax sources and administrative structure for carrying out welfare functions, and the particular individuals within the state who will receive aid. Permissive or restrictive policies of the state legislature can greatly influence the extent to which a state's citizens are to benefit from public programs, whether funded from national or state sources. The manner in which the state chooses to exercise these powers gives it a prime responsibility for distributing costs and allocating rewards within its boundaries. It is within this framework that the present volume will attempt to describe the nature of state legislatures and the manner in which they carry out their tasks.

[27] See V. O. Key, Jr., *American State Politics*, p. 4.

II APPORTIONMENT AND ELECTIONS

In 1962 the United States Supreme Court began what has subsequently been called "the reapportionment revolution."[1] Its decision in *Baker* v. *Carr*[2] has led to fundamental changes in the balance of power between the national government and the states, between the judiciary and the legislature, and between urban and rural interests. This chapter will attempt to assess the impact of the Court's action on American state legislatures, and it will discuss the relevance of reapportionment to their future. Particularly important for such a discussion will be an evaluation of the long-standing claim by reformers that reapportionment will *alter the nature of public policy*. In addition, we will comment on the nature of election systems in the states and the manner in which they influence legislative recruitment.

HISTORICAL BACKGROUND OF THE "REAPPORTIONMENT REVOLUTION"

Of the thirteen original states, six required that representation in both houses of the legislature be based essentially on population. Thirty of the

[1] Gordon E. Baker, *The Reapportionment Revolution* (New York: Random House, 1966).

[2] 396 U.S. 186 (1962).

thirty-seven states subsequently admitted to the Union originally also required representation based on population.[3] The stress on representation based on population was closely associated with the extension of the franchise in the movement toward greater democratization prior to the Civil War. Even where the apportionment provided for some minimum representation of subdivisions regardless of size, as in several New England states, representation was not greatly at variance with population, for the nation was overwhelmingly rural. As increased industrialization led to the growth of larger cities in the late nineteenth century, however, the trend toward a greater disparity between population and representation became more intense. States did not simply fail to reapportion state legislatures in accordance with population changes; rather, state after state amended its constitution to provide for other bases of representation. Rural interests sought to maintain their dominance within the states over the fast increasing labor and ethnic groups in cities. Typical provision in a state constitution guaranteed a minimum of representation to counties, regardless of size, or imposed a maximum of representation on one or more major cities. By 1963 only nine states still maintained population as the constitutional basis of representation in both houses of the state legislature. And even those states whose constitutions called for apportionment based on population did not always achieve that standard, for legislatures sometimes failed to carry out the constitutional requirement.

As the United States moved from being overwhelmingly rural to three-fifths urban, the divergence between population and representation became greater. The California senate was an extreme example, frequently cited: one senator represented more than six million people in Los Angeles County, while another represented fourteen thousand people in a sparsely populated mountain district. But the Supreme Court's historic *Baker* v. *Carr* decision was a direct result of the situation in Tennessee, where one-third of the voters elected two-thirds of the legislators.

As the discrepancy between representation and population became more pronounced in the states, attempts were made by city governments and by interest groups such as the League of Women Voters to compel reapportionment in the states through judicial action. Most courts refused to act, however, and often cited what they regarded as the controlling opinion in *Colgrove* v. *Green*.[4] In this case, which concerned congressional districts in Illinois, three justices had ruled that reapportionment was a political issue that was not justiciable.

Accordingly, when urban interests in Tennessee had exhausted all possible state remedies and then attempted to bring about reapportionment by introducing a case to the U. S. District Court, this court made the customary decision that it lacked jurisdiction.[5] On appeal, however, the United States Supreme Court heard oral arguments on

[3] Baker, *The Reapportionment Revolution*, p. 20.
[4] 328 U.S. 549 (1946).
[5] 179 F. Supp. 824 (M.S. Tenn. 1959).

the case twice and then announced its opinion in March of 1962. By a 6 to 2 vote, the Court ruled that apportionment of state legislatures was a justiciable issue, that U. S. Courts had jurisdiction, and that the appellants had standing to bring their allegation of a denial of the Fourteenth Amendment's guarantee of equal protection of the law.[6] This decision in *Baker* v. *Carr* began a fundamental revision of reapportionment of state legislatures, although it did not provide any guidelines to the U. S. Court to which the case was remanded, and it further revealed considerable differences among the members of the Supreme Court when six of the eight participants wrote opinions.

The standards for reapportionment were set out much more clearly in six decisions announced by the United States Supreme Court in June, 1964. In the first of these cases, *Reynolds* v. *Sims,* the Court ruled that the apportionment of the Alabama Legislature was invalid.[7] The decision stated clearly that both houses of a bicameral state legislature must be based on population. The Court specifically rejected the federal analogy in which one house is based on population and the other house is based on geographic units.

Justice Warren wrote:

Legislators represent people, not trees or acres. Legislators are elected by voters, not farms or cities or economic interests. As long as ours is a representative form of government, and our legislators are those instruments of government elected directly by and directly representative of the people, the right to elect legislators in a free and unimpaired fashion is a bedrock of our political system.

The Court's decision recognized that it would be impossible to establish absolute equality of population in legislative districts, but preferred to allow lower courts to work out more definite criteria for apportioning the districts on a case-by-case basis.

By holding that as a federal constitutional requisite both houses of a state legislature must be apportioned on a population basis, we mean that the Equal Protection Clause requires that a state make an honest and good faith effort to construct districts, in both houses of its legislature, as nearly of equal population as is practicable. We realize that it is a practical impossibility to arrange legislative districts so that each one has an identical number of residents, or citizens, or voters. Mathematical exactness or precision is hardly a workable constitutional requirement.

...Lower courts can and assuredly will work out more concrete and specific standards for evaluating state legislative apportionment schemes in the context of actual litigation. For the present, we deem it expedient not to attempt to spell out precise constitutional tests. What is marginally permissible in one state may be unsatisfactory in another, depending on the particular circumstances of the case.

[6]369 U.S. 186 (1962).
[7]377 U.S. 533 (1964).

Some of the general considerations that the Supreme Court mentioned were the following:

A state may legitimately desire to maintain the integrity of various political subdivisions, insofar as possible, and provide for compact districts of contiguous territory in designing a legislative apportionment scheme. Valid considerations may underlie such aims. Indiscriminate districting, without any regard for political subdivision or natural or historical boundary lines, may be little more than an open invitation to partisan gerrymandering. Single member districts may be the rule in one state, while another state might desire to achieve some flexibility by creating multimember or floterial districts....

The case of *Lucas* v. *Colorado General Assembly*, decided the same day as *Reynolds* v. *Sims* on the invalid apportionment of the Alabama Legislature, made explicit the principle that U.S. Courts were protecting the right of the individual citizen.[8] In the *Colorado* case, a majority of voters had approved an apportionment for one house that deviated somewhat from a strictly population basis and had simultaneously rejected a proposal that would apportion both houses on a population basis. Here the Court held that "an individual's constitutionally protected right to cast an equally weighted vote cannot be denied even by a vote of a majority of a state's electorate."

These decisions by the United States Supreme Court had repercussions in every state in the union. From the Court's decision in *Baker* v. *Carr* in March, 1962, until its decision in *Reynolds* v. *Sims* in June, 1964, twenty-eight states reapportioned at least one house of their legislatures. A year-and-a-half after the decision concerning the Alabama Legislature, further reapportionment of at least one house had taken place in thirty-six states. By the end of 1965 only three states had not been reapportioned since the census of 1960, and reapportionment action was pending in each of these states. A number of states had reapportioned only one house on a population basis after the *Baker* v. *Carr* decision and thus were compelled to reapportion the other house after the *Reynolds* v. *Sims* decision. Courts were increasingly active in bringing about reapportionment after *Reynolds* v. *Sims*. In seven states one or both houses were reapportioned by the courts.

State legislators were highly critical of the United States Supreme Court after its decision in *Baker* v. *Carr*. The Assembly of the States, sponsored by the Council of State Governments, recommended calling a convention to amend the United States Constitution to withdraw jurisdiction over state legislative reapportionment from U.S. Courts.[9]

Far more violent criticism greeted the Supreme Court's decision in *Reynolds* v. *Sims*. The majority in Congress was opposed to the Court's decision. At the end of 1964 the House of Representatives passed a bill that would have withdrawn jurisdiction on legislative reapportionment from the U.S. Courts, and the Senate passed a "sense of Congress"

[8]377 U.S. 713 (1964).
[9]*State Government*, Winter (1963), pp. 12–13.

resolution urging that the courts defer action in order to give the states relief from court intervention until a constitutional amendment could be passed. At the close of the 88th Congress in 1964 neither house had acted on the proposal passed by the other house.

In 1965 and 1966, under the leadership of Senator Dirksen (R-Illinois), further efforts were made to modify the Court's decisions. Senator Dirksen was twice successful in obtaining a majority, but not the required two-thirds vote, for a constitutional amendment that would have permitted a state to apportion one house of its legislature on a basis other than population. What the *Congressional Quarterly* called "the third and probably final campaign to overturn the Supreme Court's 'one-man, one-vote' ruling" was defeated in the Senate in April, 1966, by a vote of 55 to 38 — seven votes less than the two-thirds necessary for adoption.[10] Because nearly all the states had reapportioned in accordance with population in 1966, it seems unlikely that the Dirksen proposal could ever again command a majority in the Senate.

Accordingly, the principle of apportionment of both houses of state legislatures on a population basis is a clearly established principle of the American constitutional system. But however clear this principle now is, it does not deal with all the problems of apportionment. Nor does this principle make clear what the results of an apportionment system may be. We shall deal with these questions in the next sections of this chapter.

PROBLEMS OF APPORTIONMENT

The first set of problems concerns which agency will reapportion legislative districts. In the prevailing American pattern, the state constitution has delegated this task to the legislature itself. Each house has customarily determined its own apportionment, and the other house has accepted it. The result of this arrangement, however, is that legislators simply fail to act, because they have their own institutional interests that make them unwilling to deprive their own members of seats. Partisan factors further complicate these decisions. When one party dominates both houses, it may attempt to draw lines in order to gerrymander for its own advantage. When the legislature is divided, partisan differences may result in a deadlock.

Twelve states have devised other methods of reapportionment. Seven states have removed the authority for reapportionment from the legislature and have assigned it to executive officers, boards, or commissions. Five states have made provisions to assign the function to other agencies if the legislature fails to act.

Nonlegislative agencies do not encounter the difficulties of dealing with their own institutional interests, but they may have some of the other problems familiar to the legislators. When the task of apportion-

[10] *Congressional Quarterly Weekly Report*, April 15, 1966, p. 819.

ment is assigned to partisan officials, they may devise systems advanta-
geous to their own party. When the task is assigned to a commission
equally divided between representatives of both major parties, they
may be deadlocked. The failure of such a commission to reach agreement in Illinois led to at-large elections for the House of Representatives in 1964. Michigan goes a step further, therefore, and provides
that the state supreme court may choose among competing plans if
Michigan's commission cannot reach agreement. Four members from
each party comprise the commission.

Although it has not been common for American state constitutions to
assign reapportionment authority to courts, they have assumed this
right since *Baker* v. *Carr.* By the end of 1965, courts reapportioned one
or more houses in seven states. The Wisconsin supreme court was the
first court to undertake this task when differences between a Democratic governor and a Republican legislature led to a deadlock in
1964.[11] The result of this court's order may illustrate a set of problems
as serious as population malapportionment. Wisconsin, along with
Massachusetts, was uniquely apportioned on the basis of population
according to the 1950 census. Accordingly, the only basic change in the
balance of power — required reassignment of four of the 100 seats in
the assembly, and a corresponding shift in senate seats, which were
based roughly on a formula of one senate seat per three assembly seats.
The court, however, using population statistics almost exclusively,
ordered an apportionment that modified legislative apportionment in
almost all parts of the state and thus disregarded traditional commu-
nities of interest and county and local lines.[12] For example, a suburb of
less than 10,000 population was divided into three different assembly
districts and three different senate districts, which were composed
primarily of wards in Milwaukee. Parts of some counties were added to
parts of other counties, creating considerable confusion among voters,
who did not know in which districts they were to vote. Attention has so
long been directed to the lack of population apportionment that little
consideration has been given to problems that may be created by
strictest apportionment by population. The action of the Wisconsin
supreme court opened up a new set of issues that will attract more
attention in the future.

There are problems in apportionment, regardless of whether it is
done by the legislature, executives, boards, or courts; but more fundamental theoretical issues are involved in the United States Supreme
Court's emphasis on numbers alone. As Robert G. Dixon, Jr., has
argued, "the court may have transformed one of the most intricate,
fascinating, and elusive problems of democracy into a simple exercise
of applying elementary arithmetic to census data."[13] The question he

[11] State *ex rel. Reynolds* v. *Zimmerman,* 23 Wis. (2d) 606 (1964).

[12] State *ex rel. Reynolds* v. *Zimmerman,* 23 Wis. (2d) 606 (1964).

[13] Robert G. Dixon, Jr., "Reapportionment: What the Court Didn't Do," *The Reporter,*
October 8, 1964, pp. 39–41. See also Howard D. Hamilton, ed., *Reapportioning Legislatures: A Consideration of Criteria and Computers* (Columbus, Ohio: Charles E. Merrill, 1966).

raises is whether simple arithmetic should be applied to the drawing of districts, rather than taking into consideration the existence of regional, economic, or other groupings that may have special significance. U.S. Senator Everett Dirksen and other of the Court's critics have felt that special groupings such as farm areas, mining regions, or suburbs should have protected status in the states' districting plans. The Supreme Court insists, to the contrary, that the location of particular groups should not be used to draw district maps.

One of the problems that Dixon mentions concerns representation of political interests in a multimember constituent assembly chosen on the basis of wholly *geographic* districts. Here he cites a Maryland example in which a proposed reapportionment based on districts of equal population worsened the position of the underrepresented suburbs that had initiated the action to bring about reapportionment. On the other hand, some minority groups may be overrepresented if they hold the balance of power in a number of equal districts. Or, similarly, equal population may be used to create multimember districts that deprive minority groups of representation which they might achieve in single-member districts. Dixon cites Republicans and Negroes in southern cities as examples of groups that could elect members in single-member districts but not in multimember districts.

Even when a single-member district system is used exclusively, district lines can be drawn to maximize the representation of certain groups. The most obvious example in northern metropolitan areas exists in core cities with Democratic majorities and adjacent suburbs with Republican majorities. A districting system that draws out lines like spokes from the central cities, to include suburbs, may prevent Republicans from electing any representatives, whereas a districting system that creates separate suburban districts may allow the minority Republicans to elect some members. The use of the former system in Wayne County, Michigan, resulted in a situation in which the Republican 40 per cent of the voters achieved no representatives in the Michigan Legislature. And controversy on a related issue concerning the relationship of Chicago and the Cook County suburbs prevented bipartisan agreement on reapportionment in Illinois.

Courts have been less willing to enter this political thicket of group representation than they have been to decide on matters of equal population, which lends itself to simple arithmetical decisions. On the same day that the United States Supreme Court invalidated the Georgia apportionment of congressional districts on the ground that they varied too greatly in population,[14] it refused to invalidate congressional districting in New York City on an allegation of racial and ethnic gerrymandering. In this case, the New York Republicans had carved out a "Silk Stocking" district composed primarily of whites who were separated from the majority of Negroes and Puerto Ricans in adjacent areas. Noting that the districts were relatively equal in population, the

[14]*Wesberry* v. *Sanders,* 376 U.S. 1 (1964).

Court held there was inadequate proof that race was the basis of the gerrymander.[15]

Similarly, the United States Supreme Court in the following year upheld a Georgia apportionment system that provided for both single-member and multimember districts: some counties, electing more than one representative, elect them at large. It was alleged that the motive behind this provision was to prevent the election of a Negro. Although the lower U.S. Court declared this apportionment unconstitutional, the Supreme Court reversed the decision.[16] Other courts have subsequently upheld various systems of multimember districts, some of which provide that all candidates run at large; others provide that candidates must run for a particular, numbered seat.

RESULTS OF APPORTIONMENT SYSTEMS

In spite of the inordinate amount of attention and activity directed to apportionment of state legislatures since 1962, the evidence of the consequences of various apportionment systems is not conclusive. Much of the effort of those devoting strenuous activity toward achieving population apportionment has been based on assumptions for which there is no clear proof.[17]

It has been alleged, frequently, that rural legislators have not been responsive to the needs of metropolitan areas. Yet specific studies of issues indicate that when Republicans, Democrats, and representatives of core cities and their suburbs were united, they usually obtained what they wanted. Actually the evidence indicates that the principal controversies concerning metropolitan problems have been between core city and suburban representatives. In the North, the conflict is frequently between city Democrats and suburban Republicans.[18] Accordingly, the relative position of Chicago in the Illinois Legislature became worse after the 1954 apportionment, which increased suburban Cook County representation.

It has been alleged that rural legislators are reluctant to support welfare measures and other liberal policies advocated by those in urban areas. If this were the case, the most malapportioned states would have the least generous welfare systems and the lowest expenditures, but specific studies of the output of state legislatures show no correlation between policies and apportionment. Rather, the relative wealth and

[15] *Wright* v. *Rockefeller*, 376 U.S. 52 (1964).

[16] *Fortson* v. *Dorsey*, 379 U.S. 433 (1964).

[17] Gordon E. Baker, *Rural versus Urban Political Power* (New York: Random House, 1955) was an early and influential account of this and other possible consequences of apportionment. A recent anthology by Glendon Schubert, *Reapportionment* (New York: Charles Scribner's Sons, 1965), provides a broad perspective on related problems of legislative districting.

[18] David Derge, "Metropolitan and Outstate Alignments in the Illinois and Missouri Legislature Delegations," *American Political Science Review*, LIII (1959), 792–95.

the related socioeconomic factors within a state appear to be more important than either the apportionment system or partisan factors in determining welfare policies.[19]

It has been alleged that rural legislators have devised state aids and shared taxes in order to discriminate against urban areas in the distribution of state funds. The brief for appellants in *Baker* v. *Carr* stressed this factor in arguing that discrimination in the apportionment of state funds was the consequence of the discrimination against them in representation. Yet studies of particular legislation reveal that many of these financial formulae were adopted with the support of urban legislators. In any system of taxation based on ability to pay, and spending based on need, the result frequently may be that wealthy urban areas are supporting their poorer country cousins. Liberal Democrats from northern urban centers are particularly responsive to appeals for funds based on need, especially in education and welfare aids, and thus have supported equalization aids that primarily benefit rural areas.

It has been alleged that there are issues which divide rural and urban legislators so that they vote against one another on roll calls. Yet analysis of roll calls has revealed few examples of a clear-cut urban interest versus a rural interest that result in their voting against one another with a high degree of cohesion.[20] The few examples which have been found have concerned issues such as daylight saving time rather than more important issues of major public policy.[21]

It has been alleged that urban legislators associated with corrupt city machines and elected from districts in which the voters have little knowledge about them are inferior to rural legislators who are better known to their constituents. Those opposed to apportionment based on population expressed this fear and expected the quality of legislators to decline if cities were granted more representation. Yet there is no empirical evidence for this allegation. Studies of the composition of legislatures reveal no objective criteria, such as education or occupational status, which would provide evidence that urban legislators are inferior.

There remains, however, a universal conviction that apportionment

[19] Richard Hofferbert, "The Relation Between Public Policy and Some Structural and Environmental Variables in the American States," *American Political Science Review*, LX (March, 1966), 73–82; Richard Dawson and James Robinson, "Inter-Party Competition, Economic Variables, and Welfare Policies in the American States," *Journal of Politics*, XXV (May, 1963), 265–87; Thomas Dye, "Malapportionment and Public Policies in the States," *Journal of Politics*, IX (August, 1965), 586–601; David Brady and Douglas Edmonds, *The Effects of Malapportionment on Policy Output in the American States* (Iowa City, Iowa: Laboratory for Political Research, 1966).

[20] Murray Havens, *City versus Farm?* (University, Alabama: University of Alabama Press, 1957); Samuel C. Patterson, "Dimensions of Voting Behavior in a One-Party State Legislature," *Public Opinion Quarterly*, XXVI (Summer, 1962), 185–200; Thomas A. Flinn, "An Outline of Ohio Politics," *Western Political Quarterly*, XIII (1960), 719.

[21] Robert S. Friedman, "The Urban-Rural Conflict Revisited," *Western Political Quarterly*, XIV (June, 1961), 481–95, and Wilder Crane, Jr., "Do Representatives Represent?" *Journal of Politics*, XXII, No. 2 (May, 1960), 295.

does have significant consequences. Perhaps the consequences are more subtle and difficult to detect than the crass allegations discussed above. Perhaps rural legislative leadership is able to prevent some issues from coming to roll calls through the manipulation of committees or determination of the legislative calendar. Perhaps urban interests have not raised some issues simply because their cause appeared hopeless. If the reapportionment revolution does not result in drastic changes in welfare and education aids, perhaps it will result in changes such as more liberal liquor regulations or, in the South, less legislative resistance to racial integration. Moreover, there is much better evidence that apportionment affects the partisan results of elections and the balance of power within the two major parties.

Outside the South, until the census of 1950, most reapportionment campaigns were based on a demand that representation from Democratic cities should be increased at the expense of Republican rural areas. Then the census of 1960 made clear that the suburbs were the fastest growing areas, while cities such as Chicago and New York were suffering relative declines in population. Because Republicans have been more successful in dormitory suburbs and have lost support in midwestern farm areas, they are no longer so resistant to reapportionment.[22] In the South, on the other hand, Republicans have been more successful in urban areas than in the more traditional rural areas. There are also pockets of Republicanism in the mountains of eastern Kentucky and East Tennessee, and the adjoining sections of Virginia, North Carolina, and Georgia, where they were also discriminated against in their representation. Thus, reapportionment as such is not an issue dividing the political parties; rather the partisan issues revolve around the specifics of particular reapportionment proposals.

Within political parties, the apportionment system affects the balance of power and may greatly affect the party's prospects for winning elections. For example, an apportionment system may result in one party's domination in rural areas and the other party's domination in urban areas, even though each party has considerable strength where it is a minority. In Michigan, for example, the apportionment system resulted in Democratic dominance in Detroit and Republican dominance outstate, despite sizeable numbers of Republican votes in Detroit and Democratic votes elsewhere. The result of such a situation was that urban Republicans and rural Democrats did not have the strength within their legislative parties to which a system of proportional representation would have entitled them. As Malcolm Jewell pointed out, this situation may create problems for a party's candidate seeking statewide office.[23] If his party's strength and legislative record is based on rural interests, the party's candidate for governor may have prob-

[22] A Republican National Committee analysis of apportionment was written by William B. Prendergast, "Memorandum on Congressional Districting," in Glendon Schubert, ed., *Reapportionment* (New York: Charles Scribner's Sons, 1965), pp. 201–4.

[23] Malcolm E. Jewell, *The State Legislature: Politics and Practice* (New York: Random House, 1962).

lems in appealing for the urban votes he needs to win a statewide election.

Thus it appears that apportionment systems have partisan consequences and may have policy consequences, but far more research is needed in this area to be able to spell out more precisely what they are.

ELECTION SYSTEMS

There are many differences in the election systems used to choose the members of the fifty American legislatures. These differences can have a significant impact on the outcome of elections.

Forty-eight states elect their legislators on a partisan basis. Two states (Nebraska and Minnesota) elect their legislators on a nonpartisan basis; but the evidence is clear that Minnesota's nonpartisanship simply denies voters knowledge of the affiliations of the candidates, for the conservative and liberal caucuses in the legislature operate like parties in competitive states and are associated with the two major parties.[24]

Nomination of legislative candidates in direct primaries is the prevailing pattern for American state legislators. Even in states (such as New York, Connecticut, Delaware, and Indiana) that nominate candidates for statewide office at convention, candidates for the legislature are nominated in direct primaries. And primaries are also held in the two states nominating candidates on a nonpartisan basis.

Among states nominating candidates on a partisan basis, the prevalent system is the *closed primary,* in which voters are required to declare their party affiliation at the polls and receive the ballot for only that party's primary. The logic of this arrangement is to provide a means whereby the parties can decide among their membership who will represent the party at the general election. In a sense it might be considered a restriction that each voter declare his affiliation; however, the notion of "membership" in an American party is so loose that the only identifying mark distinguishing a person's partisan preferences may be a "feeling" that he is a Democrat or Republican.

In some areas, party membership is invested with more meaning. Consider, for example, large parts of the American South, where Democratic party allegiance has been predominant for over a century. In primary elections, to vote for the party of Lincoln, the Reconstruction, and the carpetbagger could be tantamount to a rejection of many of the traditions of the South. Although this sentiment has lost much of its explicit credence over the years, there remains a Democratic tradition that fosters an element of social control—Democratic allegiance being more tolerable than Republican allegiance. V. O. Key, Jr., has documented the phenomenon of "presidential Republicanism" in the South—the tendency for some voters to choose a Republican presidential candidate on the national level while voting in Democratic primaries

24 Ralph S. Fjelstad, "How About Party Labels?" *National Municipal Review,* XLIV (July, 1955), 359–64.

locally, in order to have some influence on *which* Democrat is elected.[25] In some areas of the North the closed primary has unforeseen consequences also. For example, many Republicans in Chicago complain that they may be discriminated against for jobs with the city if they vote in primaries. The precinct captains can easily obtain a list of electors in his area, to see how each voted. A person voting in the Republican primary is probably less likely to get a job or other favors through political channels if his local representatives are Democrats. Presumably the magnitude of possible inequities has diminished over the years with the decline in the power of political machines, but disadvantaged partisans (certain Chicago Republicans) are particularly sensitive to any slip in their tenuous grasp on political office.

When voters appear at the polls in the six states where the open primary is used (Alaska, Michigan, Minnesota, Montana, Utah, and Wisconsin), they receive ballots of both parties. This system makes it possible for an individual to keep his partisan identity a secret if he wishes; however, it may tend to dilute the meaning of party membership, since no public declaration is necessary. In the state of Washington, the voters are able to choose among candidates of both parties at both primary elections. Although it is difficult to establish whether crossover voting is more prevalent in open or closed primaries (or indeed whether it even exists), there is often a lingering question whether or not the members of the party with a strong, unopposed candidate in their own primary will vote in the opposition party's primary to help it select its weaker candidate. It is argued that the victory of Joseph McCarthy as the Republican nominee for U.S. Senator in the late 1940's was the result of a Democratic invasion of the Republican primary. Likewise, Wisconsin Democrats often ascribe the moderate electoral success of Alabama's George Wallace in the 1964 presidential primary to the crossover of Republicans. But regardless of the truth of either allegation, the possibility of crossover voting does provide an explanation for sometimes embarrassing situations in each party.

In ten southern states, a *runoff* primary is held if no candidate receives a majority in the initial primary. This multiple balloting is largely a result of one-party politics in which the predominant party splits into several factions, each seeking to gain office. In a fluid, multifactional party system, it may be difficult for a single candidate to gain a majority of votes because of the large number of candidates contending. As a consequence, a second election is used to resolve the contest where the first is inconclusive.[26] Another observer of party politics, Maurice Duverger, follows Key in observing that the runoff ballot may also *produce* multifactionalism in the statewide party as more candidates

---

[25] Key's classic study *Southern Politics* (New York: Alfred A. Knopf, Inc., 1949) is somewhat dated now but still useful as a reference on recent political history in the South. See Chap. 13 on Republicanism in the South, "presidential" and otherwise.

[26] See *ibid.*, Chap. 19, "The Nominating Process."

decide to take a chance in the electoral free-for-all.[27] Duverger also notes that this situation is similar to the City Council elections in New York between 1936 and 1947, when a system of proportional representation resulted in a multiplicity of parties, each gaining a measure of success because of the openness of the electoral procedure.[28]

Another variation in electoral procedure is the system of *cumulative voting* in Illinois. For the lower house of the Illinois Legislature, three persons are elected from each legislative district. The voter has three votes to cast, and he may divide them in any fashion he chooses—one vote for each of three candidates, one and one-half votes for each of two candidates, or three votes for one candidate. This procedure makes it possible for the members of the minority party to concentrate their influence on one candidate: if they consistently cast their ballots for only one man, he will be likely to win a seat. The majority party will generally put up only two candidates, to avoid splitting votes among too many contenders. The result in Illinois is that nearly each district has two representatives from the majority party and one from the minority. By tacit agreement, however, the parties often restrict the choice open to the voters: they do not run more candidates than they are certain of electing.[29]

The other forty-nine states use systems of single-member districts and multimember districts. It was once widely maintained that the American election system was basically one of single-member districts, and many explanations of the American two-party system were based on its association with single-member districts. In 1955, however, when an observer took the trouble to study state legislative districts, he found that over 45 per cent of the members of the lower houses of state legislatures were elected from multimember districts.[30] The number of representatives from multimember districts increased somewhat by 1962 and at a much faster rate after the *Reynolds* v. *Sims* decision in 1964. The courts' stress on population equality has led to more use of multimember districts, because when adjacent counties are too small and too large for one representative, it is often easiest to achieve population equality by combining counties into multimember districts.

Multimember districts are most frequently used in counties having more than one representative. This system makes it unnecessary to draw districts within counties, but it serves to add to the burden on the voter by requiring him to choose among more candidates. The voter in

---

[27] For a discussion of run-off primaries and some of their counterparts in other nations, see Duverger's *Political Parties*, translated from the French by Barbara and Robert North (New York: John Wiley & Sons, Inc., 1963), pp. 219–20. The original version of this classic book on party systems first appeared under the title *Les Partis Politiques* in 1951, published by Armand Colin.

[28] *Ibid.*

[29] George S. Blair, "Cumulative Voting: Patterns of Party Allegiance and Rational Choice in Illinois State Legislative Contests," *American Political Science Review,* LII (1958), 123–30.

[30] Maurice Klain, "A New Look at the Constituencies: The Need for a Recount and a Reappraisal," *American Political Science Review,* XLIX (December, 1955), 1105–19.

Cuyahoga County, Ohio, for example, until recently was faced with the problem of eighteen members elected at large. When counties elect many members to the legislature, large shifts in party control may result, since the several seats are likely to shift at once in party control. In a Republican year, all Republicans may be elected; the reverse may be true in a succeeding election. Also, multimember districts may be used to prevent a minority from electing representatives. Still, the courts will allow the use of this system. Another variation on this procedure is that most states require candidates to run at large; however, Arkansas, Florida, Georgia and Oregon provide that candidates run for particular numbered positions; i.e., that they contest specially designated seats.

CONCLUSION

The means of apportioning legislative seats and the manner of electing legislators both have important consequences for the functioning of the legislative system. But specifying the dimensions of these effects is not simple. In electoral systems, it has been found that the nature of the primary election, cumulative voting, proportional representation, nonpartisan elections, and multimember districts can influence the balance of partisan power in the legislature and to some extent determine which interests or groups in the state will have the most substantial voice in the creation of policy. Sometimes these various methods contain within them means for limiting the power of economic, political, or ethnic groups, and under certain conditions they may be used in a discriminatory fashion. They may also have consequences unintended by their proponents. For example, cumulative voting in Illinois often leads to a decrease rather than increase in voter choice for legislative seats; proportional representation can produce a favorable environment for minor parties (this is undoubtedly a major reason for its nonuse in legislative elections); a runoff primary may encourage party factionalism; multimember legislative districts may limit the power of minority groups. The actual policy consequences will depend largely on the nature of the political groups that achieve the most favorable power position under a given system.

In the case of legislative apportionment, though, it appears that early optimism of many political reformers has not been entirely rewarded: the assumption on the part of some that reapportionment would produce a difference in the nature of public policy output is not borne out in broad-scale comparative research.[31] In particular, it has been suggested that reapportionment would produce more equitable distributions of state moneys, more liberal welfare programs, more progressive tax schemes, and increased interparty competition. Work of social

---

[31] See footnote 19. Further citations of particular interest are: Herbert Jacob, "The Consequences of Malapportionment: A Note of Caution," *Social Forces*, XLIII (Winter, 1964), 256–61; and Thomas R. Dye, *Politics, Economics, and the Public: Policy Outcomes in the American States* (Chicago: Rand McNally & Co., 1966), in which the author examines a host of influences, including malapportionment, and their influence on public policy.

scientists in the field has not shown this to be the case. As Thomas Dye suggests in his study of public policy in the American states,

The impact of apportionment practices on policy outcomes in no way affects the moral or constitutional issues involved in state legislative reapportionment. The federal courts are committed to a policy of insuring to each citizen equal protection of apportionment laws, regardless of whether or not, or how, reapportionment affects policy outcomes.[32]

In other words, the moral and constitutional issues of apportionment policy should be considered as distinct from the actual *policy consequences* of redistricting.

Furthermore, as Duane Lockard suggests, reapportionment may have profound political implications that affect the distribution of power in the state. He argues that

The effects of malapportionment are felt in more ways than through simple rural overrepresentation; malapportionment also affects the chances that there will be divided party government between the governor and one or more houses of the legislature. Or the effects of malapportionment may be dampened by strong party leadership that persuades or pushes the overrepresented elements to go along with the policies for the sake of compiling a record for the next gubernatorial election.[33]

Thus reapportionment may have political consequences affecting the distribution of political power within a state and thereby indirectly influence the nature of public policy although its influence does not show up in the analysis of welfare expenditures and the like. And these consequences will differ from state to state.

[32] Dye, *ibid.*, p. 19.

[33] Duane Lockard, review of Herbert Jacob and Kenneth N. Vines, eds., *Politics in the American States* (Boston: Little, Brown & Co., 1965) in the *American Political Science Review*, LXI (March, 1967), 166.

III RECRUITMENT AND COMPOSITION

Having examined the institutional bases for legislative apportionment and the election of legislators, we can now turn to the recruitment process and the composition of the legislature. We shall look for answers to some important questions: How well does the model of two-party competition fit the American states? How does interparty competition affect the nature of recruitment? What sorts of people become legislators? How can they be characterized? And how do the incentives offered to the representative (notably compensation) affect the quality of the constituent assembly?

PARTY COMPETITION

The most important single variable determining the recruitment of legislators is the degree of party competition within a state and within its legislative districts. Here one encounters wide variations in the patterns of state politics. On one extreme, there are eleven southern states where the Democratic party has nearly always elected the governor during the last few decades, and minority party representation in the legislature is negligible. On the other extreme, there are ten states where neither party has dominant legislative control, and legislative majorities and gubernatorial winners have alternated on a roughly approximate basis between the two parties. Between these two extremes there are varying patterns of one-party dominance and limited two-party competition.

Although the concept is familiar to nearly everyone, determining an appropriate index or measure for the degree of interparty competition in a state is subject to diverse interpretations, usually depending upon the offices and the length of time being considered.[1] Some offices (e.g., U.S. senator or the governorship) may alternate fairly rapidly in party control while lower levels may not shift notably. On the other hand, some states may not appear competitive when a long historical period is considered, but may show recent upsurges in the strength of the minority party. Parts of the South and many areas of Republican dominance have, over recent decades, showed a general tendency to become more competitive as one-party dominance has gradually eroded.

For our purposes it appears that the best classification system is the one presented by Jewell and Patterson in *The Legislative Process in the United States*. Other studies have been based on voting patterns for President and congressmen, but the Jewell and Patterson classification is based only on state elections; namely, for governor and legislature. Because some states have been successful in insulating their politics from national trends by holding elections in off-years, and because the South notably has been characterized by the appearance of "presidential Republicans," our study of state legislatures is more meaningful in limiting its scope to state elections. Table 3–1, reproduced from their study, classifies the states by their degree of party competition for state offices during the two-decade period from 1947 to 1966.

The most important single fact that an analysis of this table reveals is the lack of two-party competition in American states. A standard, but largely inaccurate, model of American politics is one that pictures two parties of relatively equal strength competing for public office, taking turns in occupying the governorship and controlling the legislature.[2] This model is a fairly accurate representation of reality in only ten American states in the period since World War II. The majority of states are one-party states or limited two-party states where one party controlled both houses during most of the postwar years.

---

[1] The following sources contain several approaches to the measurement of interparty competition: Richard E. Dawson and James A. Robinson, "Interparty Competition, Economic Variables, and Welfare Policies in the American States," *Journal of Politics* (May, 1963), 265–89; Robert T. Golembiewski, "A Taxonomic Approach to State Political Party Strength," *Western Political Quarterly*, XI (1958), 494–513; Joseph A. Schlesinger, "A Two-Dimensional Scheme for Classifying States According to Degree of Interparty Competition," *American Political Science Review*, XLIX (1955), 1120–28; and Austin Ranney, "Parties in State Politics," in Herbert Jacob and Kenneth N. Vines, *Politics in the American States: a Comparative Analysis* (Boston: Little, Brown & Company, 1965), pp. 61–99.

[2] An effective analysis of state legislatures based on this model is Malcolm E. Jewell, *American State Legislatures: Politics and Practice* (New York: Random House, 1962). Jewell advocates this model and then demonstrates that it is not the prevailing pattern in American states.

Within states, however, one-party dominance is even more pronounced. Within those states listed as two-party states, there are many legislative districts that have always been dominated by one party.

TABLE 3–1   **STATE LEGISLATURES CLASSIFIED ACCORDING TO DEGREE OF ONE-PARTY CONTROL, 1947–1966***

A. 1. One-party States: Same party controlled the governorship and both houses throughout the period, and minority representation was negligible (all Democratic states).

| Alabama | Arkansas | Louisiana | Mississippi | South Carolina |

2. One-party States: Same party [Democratic] controlled the governorship and both houses throughout the period, and the minority representation was negligible [but Republicans were stronger here than in the group above, and this second group had developed a greater degree of two-party competitive politics].

| Florida | Georgia | North Carolina | Tennessee | Texas | Virginia |

B. States with One Party Dominant: Same party controlled both houses throughout the period but did not always control governorship, and (except for Oklahoma) minority party occasionally had over one-fourth of the seats in at least one house.

DEMOCRATIC: Arizona, Kentucky, Maryland, Oklahoma, West Virginia
REPUBLICAN: Kansas, New Hampshire, Vermont

STATE LEGISLATURES CLASSIFIED ACCORDING TO DEGREE OF TWO-PARTY COMPETITION, 1947–1966

Years of Party Control

State	Senate			House			Governorship	
	D	R	Tie	D	R	Tie	D	R

C. 1. Limited Two-party States: Same party controlled both houses throughout most of the period and the governorship at least half the time.

State	D	R	Tie	D	R	Tie	D	R
South Dakota	2	18	—	—	20	—	2	18
North Dakota	0	20	—	2	18	—	6	14
New Mexico	20	0	—	18	2	—	12	8
New York	2	18	—	2	18	—	4	16
Maine	2	18	—	2	18	—	6	14
Iowa	2	18	—	2	18	—	8	12
Wisconsin	0	20	—	4	16	—	6	14
Wyoming	0	20	—	4	14	2	8	12
Missouri	18	2	—	16	4	—	20	0
Illinois	4	16	—	4	16	—	10	10
Rhode Island	8	6	6	20	0	—	14	6
Idaho	6	14	—	2	18	—	6	14

2. Limited Two-party States: Same party controlled both houses throughout most of the period but usually not the governorship.

State	D	R	Tie	D	R	Tie	D	R
Michigan	2	18	—	2	16	2	14	6
New Jersey	0	20	—	6	14	—	12	8
Ohio	4	14	2	4	16	—	12	8

3. Limited Two party States: Two houses controlled by different parties during most of the period.

State	D	R	Tie	D	R	Tie	D	R
Nevada	0	18	2	20	0	—	12	8
Connecticut	14	6	—	2	18	—	14	6

*Alaska and Hawaii are omitted because of their brief terms as states, and Nebraska and Minnesota are omitted because they have nonpartisan legislatures. The time period is 1946–1965 for states with off-year elections: Kentucky, New Jersey, Virginia, Mississippi, and Louisiana.

TABLE 3−1 (cont.)

STATE LEGISLATURES CLASSIFIED ACCORDING TO DEGREE OF TWO-PARTY COMPETITION, 1947−1966

D. Two-party States: Neither party had dominant legislative control, and in most cases party control of legislature approximated control of governorship.

Pennsylvania	0	18	2	8	12	—	8	12
Indiana	4	16	—	6	14	—	10	10
Washington	12	6	2	16	4	—	10	10
Massachusetts	8	10	2	16	4	—	10	10
Delaware	14	6	—	12	8	—	10	10
Colorado	6	14	—	10	10	—	12	8
Oregon	8	10	2	8	12	—	2	18
California	8	10	2	8	12	—	10	10
Utah	10	10	—	8	10	2	4	16
Montana	10	10	—	10	10	—	4	16

From Malcolm E. Jewell and Samuel C. Patterson, The Legislative Process in the United States (New York: Random House, 1966), pp. 143−44.

Thus, even in those states where control of the legislature may shift from one party to the other, the shift results from competition in a few districts rather than from genuine competition in most districts of the states. This maintenance of one-party strength in individual districts means that noncompetitiveness is a widespread phenomenon; however, it can produce competitive politics at a higher level. If some districts always elect a Democrat or Republican as a matter of course, neither party will suffer the possibility of a total eclipse of strength as the result of a landslide for the other party; it will always have at least a corporal's guard of party faithfuls in positions of some importance. When the minority's electoral fortunes swing back in its favor, there will be at least a few of the party's representatives who can provide experience and leadership. In a sense, then, noncompetitiveness on the district level can produce favorable conditions for competitiveness on the state level. In fact, many states appear competitive in terms of statewide power, but are actually composed of two sets of safe districts—one for each party—with a few marginal districts that could favor either party, depending on the situation.

This anomalous relationship between district and statewide competitiveness is not without its hazards. Most important of these hazards is that the minority party may be controlled by the hard-core minority who are consistently returned to office. Usually that minority will not be representative of statewide trends and will therefore provide an ideological orientation that is detrimental to the party's chances in the wider political arena. Familiar examples might be urban Democrats who can resist a Republican sweep in the state, but who cannot make an effective appeal to less urban areas. Or consider the plight of a Republican organization always capable of maintaining a few rural representatives even in big Democratic years, but ill-equipped and reluctant to speak to the needs of city dwellers. The danger of thus hamstringing a political party can offset the statewide advantages to be gained from safe districts on the local level.

The amount of competitiveness in a district has a marked effect on the nature of recruitment for legislative office. It seems clear that party organizations assume a much greater importance in the recruitment of legislative candidates in competitive states than in one-party states. For instance, a study of legislators in New Jersey, Ohio, California, and Tennessee indicates that the "escalator" model of American politics is associated with a high degree of party competition.[3] The escalator model, widely believed to be the norm in American politics, pictures the political career as beginning on the lowest level of party positions and elective offices and proceeding onto higher levels of government. Wahlke and his associates found, however, that this career pattern was associated primarily with a high degree of party competition. Where there was little competition, candidates were more likely to be self-propelled or recruited by other organizations such as interest groups. And the lower the degree of party competition, the more likely it was that candidates began their political careers by running for higher offices.

The relative importance of party primaries is determined by the party's prospects for success in a given district.[4] There are likely to be far more contests in the primary of the party that has the greater chance of victory in the general election. Over a long period of time, ambitious politicians tend to gravitate toward the majority party and eschew the opportunity to lead the minority to defeat. Interest in elections would therefore tend to concentrate in the primary of the dominant party where, in some areas, turnout may exceed that of the general election, because winning the majority party's primary is tantamount to victory. Where there is virtually no competition between parties, then, primary contesting will be probably stronger in the majority party.[5] Furthermore, the majority party may find itself unable to exert much control over the individuals who run under its label, because the meaning of the label will be diminished and the growth of intraparty factions may be encouraged.

It is therefore in districts with minimal competition that party organizations may have the least trouble in recruiting men for office; but it may also have considerable difficulty specifying *who* should get the party's nomination. Where the minority's prospects appear hopeless, the party organization itself is more likely to assume an active role in recruiting its candidates. In these districts, the minority party may need to twist someone's arm to obtain a name to place on the ballot. On the other hand, candidates of the majority party are more likely to be self-starters or to be recruited by groups other than the party.

In addition, the primary election itself removes some of the power of party organizations to choose candidates. The primary was intended to

---

[3] John C. Wahlke, Heinz Eulau, William Buchanan, and LeRoy C. Ferguson, *The Legislative System: Explorations in Legislative Behavior* (New York: John Wiley & Sons, Inc., 1962), p. 96.

[4] V. O. Key, *American State Politics* (New York: Alfred A. Knopf, Inc., 1956), pp. 97–118.

[5] See William H. Standing and James A. Robinson, "Interparty Competition and Primary Contesting: The Case of Indiana," *American Political Science Review*, LXII (1958), 1066–77.

remove nomination politics from back rooms and caucuses. To the extent that it has, party organizations find it difficult to exert control over candidate selection. In some areas, the party may try to re-assert its prerogatives by calling a pre-primary convention in which the members of the organization agree on a list of names to be presented on the primary ballot, but even this tactic has its limitations and does not restore the power of candidate selection to the party apparatus. Thus, because of the primary and the influences of competition, parties are not notably effective in performing their recruitment function in many parts of the nation.

COMPOSITION

Members of American state legislatures are not representative of the population from which they are elected. Women and minority groups are not represented in accordance with their numbers, and legislators everywhere have a higher socioeconomic status than the population that they represent.

Although the American population has become increasingly mobile, the majority of American legislators were born, or have lived most of their lives, in the districts from which they were elected. Table 3–2 from the Wahlke study indicates that even in California, with its mass influx of migrants since World War II, the majority of legislators had lived thirty years or 80 per cent of their lives in their districts. In the highly mobile society of twentieth century America, the *least* mobile (in a geographical sense) are those who are entrusted with minding the store politically. Policy is made by those who are most likely to be localistic, while many of those who are likely to gain a broader perspective are less effective because of their transience and inability to meet the tacit requirement of long-term local residence. The characteristic most likely to be shared by the movers and nonmovers, however, is upward *social* mobility, or at least a general middle-class social and economic position. If this is true, then many of the political demands of the geographically mobile part of society may find legislative expression even though their political participation may be limited.

TABLE 3–2		RESIDENCE IN DISTRICT		
Length of residence in district	Calif. N = 118	N.J. N = 79	Ohio N = 162	Tenn. N = 119	Total N = 488
"All my life"	14%	60%	65%	53%	48%
Most (80%) of life, or over 30 years	42	23	23	23	28
20–29 years	15	7	7	11	10
10–19 years	19	10	3	9	10
Less than 10 years	10	—	2	4	4
	100%	100%	100%	100%	100%

From Wahlke et al., The Legislative System; Explorations in Legislative Behavior (New York: John Wiley & Sons, Inc., 1962), p. 488.

TABLE 3-3   **OCCUPATIONS OF FATHERS OF AMERICAN LEGISLATORS**
(in percentages)

Occupation	Calif., N.J., Ohio, Tenn. (1957)	Wis. (1957)	Pa. (1957)	U.S. senators (1947-57)	Labor force (1900)
Professional	18	17	12	24	6
Proprietor, official	29	14	30	35	7
Farmer, farm manager	31	25	16	32	22
Other	28	38	42	9	66
Total	100	100	100	100	100
Numbers	504	100	106	180	—

From Jewell and Patterson, The Legislative Process in the United States *(New York: Random House, 1966), p. 104, where the following sources were credited: J. C. Wahlke et al.,* The Legislative System *(New York: John Wiley and Sons, 1962), p. 489; F. J. Sorauf,* Party and Representation *(New York: Atherton Press, 1963), p. 78; D. R. Matthews, "United States Senators: A Collective Portrait,"* International Social Science Journal, *XIII (1961), 623.*

All studies of American legislators indicate that they come from socioeconomic backgrounds higher than those of the majority of the population. In Table 3-3, occupations of legislators' fathers are compared with the work force of 1900, indicating that the majority of legislators had fathers who were professionals, proprietors, officials, or farmers. The status of legislators' fathers was not quite as high as that of the fathers of U.S. senators, but it clearly differentiated them from the general work force in 1900 (a rough approximation of the birth date of many of the legislators).

The occupations of the legislators themselves indicate that they are upwardly mobile and that they overrepresent higher status occupations. Table 3-4 indicates that less than 10 per cent of state legislators held occupations that were the same as those held by the majority of wage earners in the country. While state legislators generally do not attain the status enjoyed by U.S. senators, for example, they do tend to outstrip their fathers and large numbers of their contemporaries.

TABLE 3-4   **OCCUPATION OF LEGISLATORS' FATHERS, LEGISLATORS THEMSELVES, U.S. SENATORS, AND THE U.S. LABOR FORCE, 1950**

Occupation	Legislators' Fathers	Legis- lators	Senators*	Labor Force, 1950†
Professional, technical	18%	47%	64%	7%
Proprietors, managers, officials	29	35	29	7
Farmers, farm managers	25	10	7	16
Craftsmen, foremen, operatives	16	2	—	31
Clerical, sales	5	5	—	15
Unskilled labor, servants, farm labor	5	—	—	20
Other, not known	2	1	—	4
	100%	100%	100%	100%

*Donald R. Matthews, U.S. Senators and Their World (Chapel Hill: University of North Carolina Press, 1960), p. 282.
†From Wahlke, et al., op.cit., p. 489. Statistical Abstract, 1957, pp. 219-20.

TABLE 3−5   **EDUCATIONAL LEVEL OF AMERICAN LEGISLATORS**
(in percentages)

Education	Calif. (1957)	N.J. (1957)	Ohio (1957)	Tenn. (1957)	Wis. (1957)
Elementary only	−(33)	−(47)	4(43)	4(60)	8(52)
Some high school	15(45)	13(38)	19(42)	22(29)	24(34)
Some college	31(11)	24 (6)	19 (7)	28 (6)	23 (7)
College graduate	54 (8)	63 (7)	58 (6)	46 (4)	45 (5)
Total	100	100	100	100	100
Numbers	120	79	162	120	100

NOTE: Numbers in parentheses indicate proportions of the total relevant populations in each category.
From Jewell & Patterson, op cit., p. 108, where the following sources were credited: J. C. Wahlke et al., The Legislative System (New York: John Wiley and Sons, 1962), p. 489; W. P. Tucker, "Characteristics of State Legislators," Social Science, XXX (1955), 94−98; K. Janda et al., Legislative Politics in Indiana (Bloomington, Ind: Indiana University Press, 1961), p. 3; M. M. McKinney, "The Personnel of the Seventy-seventh Congress," American Political Science Review, XXXVI (1942), 70; D. R. Matthews, "United States Senators: A Collective Portrait," International Social Science Journal, XIII (1961), 625; F. J. Sorauf, Party and Representation (New York: Atherton Press, 1963), p. 69; H. M. Thomason, "The Legislative Process in Georgia" (unpublished Ph.D. dissertation, Emory University, 1961), pp. 82−83.

Professional, technical occupations were the largest single group, and proprietors, managers, officials, and farmers were greatly overrepresented.

Lawyers are the largest single occupational group identifiable in state legislatures. Although the percentage of lawyers in state legislatures has never been as high as in Congress, they have always had representation far exceeding their fraction of 1 per cent of the population, and their percentage appears to be increasing.[6] Of the other business occupations represented in state legislatures, a large number are real estate dealers, insurance agents, and others who may be described as bargainers and negotiators, occupationally trained to represent other persons and to compromise interests in order to reach agreement with others.[7]

Although much attention has been directed to the large percentage of lawyers in state legislatures, there is little evidence that this occupational status affects decisions.[8] It may be that lawyers, occupationally

[6] Malcolm E. Jewell and Samuel C. Patterson, The Legislative Process in the United States (New York: Random House, 1966), pp. 107, 109.

[7] Wahlke *et al., op. cit.,* p. 243.

[8] David R. Derge, "The Lawyer as a Decision-Maker in the American State Legislature," *Journal of Politics,* XXI (1959), 408−33; Jewell and Patterson, *op. cit.,* pp. 107−11; David Gold, "Lawyers in Politics: An Empirical Exploration of Biographical Data on State Legislators," *Pacific Sociological Review,* IV (1961), 85; Leonard Ruchelman, "Lawyers in the New York State Legislature: The Urban Factor," *Midwest Journal of Political Science,* X (November, 1966), 484−97; Heinz Eulau and John D. Sprague, *Lawyers in Politics: A Study in Occupational Convergence* (Indianapolis: Bobbs-Merrill Company, Inc., 1964), a book-length treatment of lawyers in legislative politics derived from the four-state study by Wahlke and associates.

TABLE 3–5 (Cont.)

Minn. (1951)	Ind. (1961)	Pa. (1958)	Ga. (1961)	U.S. House (1941–43)	U.S. Senate (1947–57)
(50) 23	7(46)	10(42)	12(50)	*	1(48)
(34)	20(41)	39(45)	26(37)	9	14(38)
23 (9)	26 (6)	15 (6)	32 (7)	3	84(14)
54 (6)	47 (5)	36 (6)	40 (6)	88	
100	100	100	100	100	99
n.a.	99	106	259	431	180

*Less than 1%.

trained to represent others, are more effective in representing workers than a worker himself would be. Because very few legislators list working-class occupations as their vocation, it appears that representation of the interests of labor, however defined, is achieved largely through representatives who are from laboring backgrounds but have gained higher socioeconomic status, who must nurture the support of labor to gain election, or who are ideologically oriented to those interests; otherwise, that occupational stratum does not contribute significantly to the membership of most state legislatures.

The contrary is true for farmers. Although their percentage in state legislatures has declined for some years, farmers have generally had a higher proportion of representatives in the assembly than their proportion in the electorate. Reapportionment in the mid-1960's has probably resulted in further decrease in the number of members who claim to be farmers.

In addition to the relatively high occupational status of legislators compared to the general populations they represent, educational achievement is also much higher. As Table 3–5 indicates, the majority of legislators have attended college, even in Tennessee where 60 per cent of the population has not advanced beyond an elementary education. This characteristic would be expected simply because of the high proportion of lawyers in most legislatures; however, high educational attainment is also prevalent among the professional and business membership, which also contributes a large number of legislators. Thus, only a limited segment of the population is "eligible" for legislative membership if recent history is an indication of the informal requirements necessary for attaining a seat in the representative body.[9]

[9] This finding with respect to state legislatures is consistent with Donald R. Matthews' study of the backgrounds of U.S. senators. In his book, *U.S. Senators and Their World* (Chapel Hill: University of North Carolina Press, 1960), he suggests that only a minuscule proportion of the population—perhaps 5 per cent—is eligible for membership in the Senate according to its recent composition (see especially Matthews' Chap. 2). Undoubtedly this percentage would be larger for state legislators, but the point is established that they do not mirror the over-all distribution of occupation and status in their general populations. For an explicit comparison of occupational representation in state legislatures and Congress, see also Donald R. Matthews, *The Social Background of Political Decision-Makers* (New York: Random House, 1954), p. 30.

In his study of the Pennsylvania Legislature, Frank Sorauf finds that a systematic influence produces this emphasis on status and occupational standing. In the first place, it is argued, candidates must fulfil certain "birthright" requirements of the constituency; namely, reflections of dominant ethnic, religious, or racial origins in the district. This can be considered a threshold for acceptability. An Italian mother, a father who works in a factory, a Polish name, white-Anglo-Saxon-Protestant (WASP) family, proper religious affiliation—any of these background characteristics can serve as an asset in the right district; in others it might be the "kiss of death." However, beyond these basics, Sorauf suggests that the candidate should have risen above his origins. As he puts it,

Paradoxically, voters seem to want both the typical and atypical in their elected representatives. In certain characteristics—religion, race, ethnic background—they compel the parties to select candidates in their own images. Yet they favor candidates with education, occupation, and general social status far above the average. They seek the successful, the respected man—the common man write large, so to speak. What they get, given both their demands and the opportunities of political life, are often ambitious, upward-mobile representatives of the background and parentage typical of large numbers of voters in the district.[10]

In spite of the fact that legislative seats are not often the most coveted jobs available in the district, it is likely that successful candidates will possess backgrounds that are common, but status which is coveted.

It has also been found that the early political socialization of legislators—attitudes and perceptions of politics they obtained while young—also differentiate representatives from their constituents. Wahlke and his associates suggest that legislators, often with relatives in politics, may have been impelled into the political arena because of this early exposure.[11] The fact that one may also have a good "political" name will often be relevant to his career, especially if there is a record of public service or public officeholding associated with the family name.

TENURE AND TURNOVER

A striking characteristic of state legislative service is the high rate of turnover. In contrast with the low rate of attrition in Congress (where only a fraction of the membership is replaced in a normal election), state legislators serve for short periods. There are states in which the majority of members in the lower house are first-term members.

Charles Hyneman, who did the first thorough study of state legislative turnover, argued that it took three or four sessions for a legislator to acquire the experience necessary to be effective. Yet, in the period from 1925 to 1935, only 20 per cent of the members had served for

---

[10] Frank J. Sorauf, *Party and Representation* (New York: Atherton Press, 1963), p. 81.
[11] Wahlke *et al., op. cit.,* Chap. 4.

four sessions in the ten states that he studied.[12] There is some evidence that there has been a decline in turnover since Hyneman wrote; but there are still states with a majority of new members in both houses.[13]

The argument is often made, therefore, that new arrivals come to the legislature with little experience in lawmaking, and that increased tenure would increase the "quality" of state legislators. The assumption is that longer service will give the individual more opportunity to become skilled at his tasks and, more importantly, to gain more *expertise*, allowing him to make better judgments and to act as a check on the executive. A high rate of attrition in the legislative membership, it is argued, reduces the level of performance of both the lawmaking and watchdog functions of a representative body.

Another possible consequence of rapid turnover is suggested by Duane Lockard in his study of politics in New England. He observes that in the state of Connecticut, the influx of new members actually strengthens the existing legislative party organizations because the newcomers must conform to leadership demands in order to gain a hearing for their own policy preferences.[14] Where an existing organization may control the outcome of bills that the new legislator may wish to propose, his inexperience is likely to make him all the more susceptible to party demands.

Where the legislative parties are not cohesive, the influx of droves of new representatives may reduce party effectiveness still further and foster party irresponsibility. A legislator may not feel obliged to follow the demands of the party delegation, and he may assume an independent status. When this happens, turnover aggravates already present problems of legislative factionalism. Also, the legislator may fully intend to retire voluntarily after one or two terms and therefore work to advance some private cause which might normally lead to an involuntary retirement. In short, if the legislator does not intend to seek re-election, the element of constituency control over his behavior may not be even minimally effective; and if his party is not cohesive when he arrives, he may feel under no constraint to make it more so.

Attempts to explain the high turnover in American state legislatures usually mention such factors as reapportionment, interparty competition, and compensation (including both salary and perquisites such as staff aids). Of these influences, reapportionment is probably the least important in the long view. The 1962 and 1964 Supreme Court decisions have increased turnover as old districts have been dropped and new ones created, but this is a temporary factor and not critical to our basic question of why so many legislators serve only one or two terms.

In our discussion of party competition we have already made clear that defeat in general elections is not a very important contribution to short tenure. Even where there is competition in primaries, incumbents

---

[12] Charles S. Hyneman, "Tenure and Turnover of Legislative Personnel," *Annals of the American Academy of Political and Social Science*, CXCV (1938), pp. 21–31.

[13] Jewell and Patterson, *op. cit.*, pp. 119–20.

[14] Duane Lockard, *New England State Politics* (Princeton: Princeton University Press, 1959), p. 291.

are most likely to win, so primary defeats in one-party areas do not explain the high rate of turnover. For example, in Connecticut between 1946 and 1958 only 26 per cent of retirements from the house resulted from defeats, while incumbents won 982 times and lost only 219 times.[15]

The custom of party rotation agreements contributed to a majority of new members in each session of legislatures in southern states. Under this system, the party agreed that in a district comprised of more than one county, the candidate could not be from the same county in two successive elections. The practice is no longer permitted by the courts.

Thus, if neither institutional nor political factors explain the high rate of state legislative turnover, the explanation must be that legislators, for personal reasons, do not wish to seek re-election. Those who wish to have legislators acquire greater experience must therefore give heed to Hyneman's advice: "The state legislator must be made more happy in his career . . . ."[16]

COMPENSATION

Although compensation is not the only factor in making the state legislator happy in his career, it is of great importance. In most American states the legislators are not regarded as full-time public servants, and their compensation is therefore not enough for them to devote full time to their legislative tasks. But, as many of them complain, the legislative tasks take so much time from other pursuits that they ultimately cannot afford to continue serving.

Compensation of legislators may vary from the $200 per biennium paid New Hampshire legislators to the $15,000 annual salary of New York legislators. Payment by salary or on a per diem basis is a basic difference among states: 33 pay salaries, 14 pay per diem, 3 pay both. The median biennial salary is $4,800 and the median per diem is $15.

Table 3–6 indicates the estimated biennial compensation of state legislators. In general, states that provide a salary compensate their legislators more liberally than those that pay per diem. Those whose legislative compensation is determined by statute compensate their legislators more liberally than those restricted by constitutional provisions for specific sums. In the main, states with annual sessions compensate their legislators more liberally than those with biennial sessions, although there are exceptions, such as Rhode Island, which has annual sessions, but its constitutional provision for $5 per day restricts the compensation to $600 per biennium.

States which compensate their legislators on a daily basis usually restrict the number of days for which the legislators may collect pay.

In addition to basic compensation, thirty-seven states pay their

[15]James D. Barber, *The Lawmakers: Recruitment and Adaptation to Legislative Life* (New Haven: Yale University Press, 1965), p. 8.

[16]Hyneman, *op. cit.*, p. 30.

TABLE 3-6   **REALIZED COMPENSATION FOR A BIENNIUM OF A TYPICAL LEGISLATOR
IN SALARY, PER DIEM AND LIVING EXPENSE ALLOWANCES**
(Computed for Typical-Length Regular Sessions)(a)

State	Biennial compensation	Pay basis	State	Biennial compensation	Pay basis
New Hampshire	$ 200	S	Kentucky	$ 6,300	D(b)
Rhode Island	600(A)	D	Oklahoma	6,300(A)	S & D(b)
Utah	1,230	S(b)	Colorado	6,400(A)	S
Wyoming	1,280	D(b)	Maryland	7,300(A)	S(b)
New Mexico	1,800(A)	D	Hawaii	7,770 to	S(b)
Idaho	2,100	D(b)		9,220(c)(A)	S
Montana	2,100	D(b)	Oregon	8,400	S & D
North Dakota	2,270	D(b)	Washington	8,700	S(b)
Maine	2,380 to	S(b)	South Carolina	9,400(A)	S(b)
	2,912(c)		Louisiana	9,750(A)	D(b)
South Dakota	3,000	S	Florida	10,500	S(b)
West Virginia	3,000(A)	S	Georgia	10,525(A)	S(b)
Virginia	3,300	D(b)	Texas	11,040	S(b)
Arkansas	3,600	S & D	Minnesota	11,042 to	S(b)
Tennessee	3,600	S(d)		11,763(c)	
Arizona	3,600 to	S(b)	Delaware	11,200(A)	S(b)
	5,928(c)(A)		Missouri	11,550	S(b)
Alabama	3,780	D(b)	New Jersey	15,000(A)	S
Nevada	3,900	D(b)	Ohio	16,000	S
Connecticut	4,000	S(b)	Massachusetts	16,800(A)	S(b)
Kansas	4,000(A)	D(b)	Alaska	17,600(A)	S(b)
Vermont	4,000	S(b)	Illinois	18,000	S
North Carolina	4,200	D(b)	Wisconsin	16,800 to	S(b)
Nebraska	4,800	S		18,450(c)	
Indiana	4,820	S(b)	Pennsylvania	24,000(A)	S(b)
Iowa	5,800	D	Michigan	30,000(A)	S(b)
			New York	30,000(A)	S(d)
Mississippi	6,025	S(b)	California	35,075(A)	S(b)

Abbreviations: (A)—Annual sessions; (D)—Daily or weekly pay basis; (S)—Salary basis.
*Totals show compensation prevailing in or authorized during 1966, excluding mileage, stationery, and all variable interim allowances.
(a) Where necessary to compute pay on the basis of days or weeks of regular session, the regular sessions of 1964 and 1965 have been used.
(b) Additional expense payments are made and are included in compensation shown.
(c) The alternative figures for these States result from differential expense allowances paid to legislators who do or do not reside in or adjacent to the capital city.
(d) Legislature authorized to establish expense allowance during session. Amounts not shown in figures above.
From *American State Legislatures: Their Structures and Procedures* (Chicago: The Council of State Governments, 1967), p. 14.

legislators additional money for expenses. These expenses may include hotel bills, meals, transportation, telephone calls, stationery, and postage; however, beyond basic compensation and expenses there are few perquisites of state legislators. They have nothing comparable to the large offices and staffs of Congressmen. With such notable exceptions as California, which provides its legislators with offices and staff, most legislators must handle their business from their desks in the chambers or from their homes. In most states, only a few legislative leaders have offices and private secretarial assistance. Naturally, this general lack of staff and office assistance does not contribute to a legislator's sense of efficacy, and it provides handicaps for ambitious legislators who might be more effective in their jobs if they were given more support for their legislative tasks. With nobody to help with casework (from constituents), many state legislators literally run errands to various state agencies to seek favors and expedite business for people in their districts. The legislator finds his usefulness hampered—a particularly harmful situation today, when he needs more *expertise* to perform the increasingly complex task of making public policy.

Whether increased staff aids would decrease turnover is not clear, but they would probably increase the effectiveness of the individual legislator. Whether increased compensation would improve the quality of legislators or diminish their inclination to accept meals and drinks (or even contributions) from lobbyists would be difficult to prove. It is a fact, however, that one of the most frequently cited reasons for not seeking re-election to state legislatures is that the compensation is not great enough for the demands of the job.

LEGISLATIVE RESPONSIBILITY AND LEGISLATIVE TURNOVER

Legislators are emissaries upon whom the stamp of local culture has been placed, but who usually must occupy an above-average station in life to be tapped for service. The strong parochial bias in state legislative recruitment suggests that, for many matters, the representative will be a "walking input" of constituency demands to the legislative system—a culture carrier who will automatically transmit elements of the local political culture to the legislature.

When a legislator does not function in accord with the wishes of his constituents, his defeat is not always forthcoming, however. The constituents may not even be aware of his behavior; or he may be able to obfuscate criticism with local homilies, fish fries and block parties for constituents, political favors, or impermeable machine support. Here we assume that he likes his job as legislator and may devise means to keep it. But what if he doesn't like the job well enough to keep it for more than one or two terms? What if his motive in seeking office is to strike quickly for some special interest or favorite policy and then retire voluntarily from "public" service? In such instances, punishment by electoral defeat is not an effective chastening device and does not avail the constituents of a major means of control over representatives. If a legislator decides that the compensations of the office (e.g., prestige in the community and salary) are insufficient to hold him, he may voluntarily retire from his post and return to a law practice or business or run for a more attractive political position.

Legislators are usually socially ascending, and only a few are willing to devote as many as ten years to their office. It is possible that increased compensation of various kinds might extend tenure in state legislatures, but the problem is a fundamental one not easily solved. The office of state legislator is not at the top of a clearly defined social or economic hierarchy; it is moderately situated socially and low in the economic scale. The job does not provide a final goal for the politically ambitious; more likely, it is a halfway house for the upward bound.

In such circumstances, the process of representation takes on new proportions. In a commonly held conception of the model representative process, legislators transmit constituency demands to the legislature, vote on policy, and are removed from the office if their performance is not validated at the polls by the voters. In part, this standard conception holds true, but there are probably more aberrant than model cases. Where rapid and voluntary turnover is prevalent (and probably not likely to abate substantially in the near future), it seems that the crux of the representative process is in the parochial, localistic bias of legislators. If they indeed function as culture carriers, many demands of the constituents will be automatically injected into the legislative system, because the legislator will have absorbed much of the culture of his district. A homogeneous district without strong social or economic cleavage would be expected to produce similarly oriented legislators from one election to the next, and the representatives would therefore respond with roughly similar policies. Cultural homogeneity would be as forceful as constituency demands in controlling legislators; in fact, the representational process would be linked together by means of social control rather than overt political control. Although this conception of state legislative representation may be less pleasing (in a normative sense), it explicitly recognizes that there is considerable slippage in the elements of political control posited in the model of two-party competition.

In heterogeneous districts containing diverse social and economic subcultures, one or the other position in the electorate would be exaggerated in our winner-take-all single-member district system. If there is diversity in the district, each candidate will try to piece together a winning coalition of various interests.

Depending on the exigencies of politics, the winning coalitions may vary from year to year, thereby resulting in a succession of legislators who vary widely from each other in their policy responses. In a sense, each legislator will be representing a different "constituency" within his geographic district. A common example of this phenomenon occurs in urban districts where workers favoring liberal Democratic candidates are opposed electorally by a suburban-based managerial group possibly favoring a conservative Republican (see discussion in Chapter V). Another common pattern can be found in rural districts containing a middle-sized city: either the agrarian or urban interests might provide the winning coalition in a given year. Where the nature of competing subgroups differs widely, the nature of representation (i.e., the kind of legislator and the nature of his response to matters of public policy) will tend to change from year to year.

If the groups in heterogeneous districts such as these are well defined and have some form of organization, legislators may feel the political control that results from the attention of his winning coalition (and the attacks of the losing coalition). This political control is stronger if social and economic cleavages correspond to partisan division, because the parties will gauge their appeals to different kinds of people. In fact, partisanship and political control are likely to be the strongest where political divisions reflect deeper cleavages in the society.[17]

We would expect an element of political control to be present in heterogeneous districts, where different electoral coalitions maintain some form of organization to vie for political office. In this situation the "outs" provide a check on the "ins." In a homogeneous district, or one where the "outs" have no effective voice, social control through local norms may be the most effective guarantee of the legislator's responsibility to his constituency, particularly if it is a one-party district. Nowhere, however, will the social or political forms of influence offer a very effective means for controlling the "hit-and-run" legislator who plans no future in that office.

[17]See the text and notes in Chap. V for a discussion of the relationship between constituency influences and partisanship.

IV STRUCTURE
AND PROCEDURE

The basic structure of each state legislature is set forth in the state constitution. Forty-nine states have bicameral legislatures, and Nebraska has had a unicameral legislature since 1937. Now that both houses of state legislatures must be apportioned on the basis of population, there may be less justification for having two chambers, but the bicameral principle seems firmly established in the American states.

Twenty-six states designate their legislative bodies simply as the Legislature; others use terms such as General Assembly, Legislative Assembly, or General Court for both bodies together. Table 4–1 indicates which terminology is used in each state. The upper house in every state and the unicameral Nebraska legislature are called the senate. Forty-two of the lower houses follow the national pattern, each with the designation House of Representatives. The other seven states use the terms Assembly, General Assembly, and House of Delegates.

Table 4–2 indicates the numbers, terms, and party affiliations of legislators in August, 1965. In all states, the senate is smaller than the lower house. Senates range in size from a membership of 17 in Nevada to 67 in Minnesota, while lower houses range in size from 35 in Delaware to 400 in New Hampshire. The Nebraska senate has 49 members.

Forty-five states have two-year terms for members

TABLE 4-1   OFFICIAL NAMES OF STATES, LEGISLATIVE BODIES, AND CAPITOL BUILDINGS

State of, or other jurisdiction	Both bodies	Senate	House	Capitol building
Ala.	Legislature	S	HR	State Capitol
Alaska	Legislature	S	HR	State Capitol
Ariz.	Legislature	S	HR	State Capitol
Ark.	General Assembly	S	HR	State Capitol
Calif.	Legislature	S	Assembly	State Capitol
Colo.	General Assembly	S	HR	State Capitol
Conn.	General Assembly	S	HR	State Capitol
Del.	General Assembly	S	HR	Legislative Hall
Fla.	Legislature	S	HR	State Capitol
Ga.	General Assembly	S	HR	State Capitol
Hawaii	Legislature	S	HR	Iolani Palace
Idaho	Legislature	S	HR	State Capitol
Ill.	General Assembly	S	HR	State Capitol
Ind.	General Assembly	S	HR	(a)
Iowa	General Assembly	S	HR	State Capitol
Kan.	Legislature	S	HR	State House (b)
Ky., Commonwealth of	General Assembly	S	HR	State Capitol
La.	Legislature	S	HR	State Capitol
Me.	Legislature	S	HR	State House
Md.	General Assembly	S	House of Delegates	State House
Mass., Commonwealth of	General Court	S	HR	State House
Mich.	Legislature	S	HR	State Capitol
Minn.	Legislature	S	HR	State Capitol
Miss.	Legislature	S	HR	State Capitol
Mo.	General Assembly	S	HR	State Capitol
Mont.	Legislative Assembly	S	HR	State Capitol
Neb.	Legislature	Unicameral		State Capitol
Nev.	Legislature	S	Assembly	State Capitol
N. H.	General Court	S	HR	State House
N. J.	Legislature	S	General Assembly	State House
N. M.	Legislature	S	HR	State Capitol
N. Y.	Legislature	S	Assembly	State Capitol
N. C.	General Assembly	S	HR	State Capitol(c)
N. D.	Legislative Assembly	S	HR	State Capitol
Ohio	General Assembly	S	HR	State House (b)
Okla.	Legislature	S	HR	State Capitol
Ore.	Legislative Assembly	S	HR	State Capitol
Pa., Commonwealth of	General Assembly	S	HR	State Capitol
R. I. and Providence Plantations	General Assembly	S	HR	State House
S. C.	General Assembly	S	HR	State House
S. D.	Legislature	S	HR	State Capitol
Tenn.	General Assembly	S	HR	State Capitol
Tex.	Legislature	S	HR	State Capitol(b)
Utah	Legislature	S	HR	State Capitol
Vt.	General Assembly	S	HR	State House
Va., Commonwealth of	General Assembly	S	House of Delegates	State Capitol

TABLE 4−1 (Cont.)
OFFICIAL NAMES OF STATES, LEGISLATIVE BODIES, AND CAPITOL BUILDINGS

State of, or other jurisdiction	Both bodies	Senate	House	Capitol building
Wash.	Legislature	S	HR	Legislative Building
W. V.	Legislature	S	House of Delegates	State Capitol
Wis.	Legislature	S	Assembly	State Capitol
Wyo.	Legislature	S	HR	State Capitol
Guam	Legislature	Unicameral		Congress Building
P. R.	Legislative Assembly	S	HR	Capitol
V. I., Territory of	Legislature	Unicameral		Capitol

(a) No official name. Both "State House" and "State Capitol" used.
(b) Unofficial.
(c) Since 1963, legislature has met in its own building, "Legislative Building."
Abbreviation: S, Senate; HR, House of Representatives.
From Frank Smothers, ed., The Book of the States: 1966−67 *(Chicago: The Council of State Governments, 1966), p. 44*

of the lower house, and four states have four-year terms. Thirty-seven states have four-year terms for their state senators, while the others have two-year terms.

LEADERSHIP

Although the structural factors concerning size and terms are set forth in state constitutions, leadership (except for the common constitutional provision that the lieutenant governor shall preside over the senate) is usually determined by the formal and informal rules of each legislative body. All lower houses elect their own presiding officer, who is invariably called the speaker. Fourteen state senates also elect their presiding officer, but the prevailing pattern is that the lieutenant governor, like the Vice-President of the United States, is the presiding officer of the senate. Since a lieutenant governor, except in Tennessee, is not a member of the body over which he presides, he has less influence than an elected speaker; thus, a president pro tempore or other elected leaders are often more powerful than the lieutenant governor.

Other formal positions in the legislature include floor leaders and members of steering committees; the latter may actually become more important than regular committees by scheduling the consideration of bills, especially at the end of the session.

Formal leadership positions are not necessarily the most important in a legislative body, nor are they always held by the same people who make up the informal leadership patterns. The most important variable in legislative leadership is the degree of partisanship in a legislative body. In the one-party South, governors may exercise considerable influence in the selection of presiding officers and floor leaders. In other areas, the legislators may jealously guard their prerogatives of

TABLE 4–2 THE LEGISLATORS · Numbers, Terms, and Party Affiliations (as of August 1, 1965)

State or other jurisdiction	Senate Dem	Senate Rep	Senate Vacancies	Senate Constitutional total	Senate Term	House Dem	House Rep	House Vacancies	House Constitutional total	House Term	Constitutional total of legislators
Ala.	35	..	..	35	4	102	4	..	106	4	141
Alaska	17	3	..	20	4	30	10	..	40	2	60
Ariz.	26	2	..	28	2	45	35	..	80	2	108
Ark.	35	..	..	35	4	99	1	..	100	2	135
Calif.	25	14	1	40	4	49	31	..	80	2	120
Colo.	15	20	..	35	4	42	23	..	65	2	100
Conn.	23	13	..	36	2	111	183	..	294(a)	2	330(a)
Del.	13	5	..	18	4	30	5	..	35	2	53
Fla.	42(b)	2	..	44(b)	4	102	10	..	112	2	156(c)
Ga.	44	9	..	54(d)	2	182	23	..	205	2	259(d)
Hawaii	16	9	..	25	4	39	12	..	51	2	76
Idaho	19	25	..	44	2	37	42	..	79	2	123
Ill.	24	32	2	58	4(e)	116	58	3	177	2	233
Ind.	35	15	..	50	4	77	22	1	100	2	150
Iowa	34	25	..	59	4	101	23	..	124	2	183
Kan.	13	27	..	40	4	44	81	..	125	2	165
Ky.	24	13	1	38	4	62	37	1	100	2	138
La.	38	..	1	39	4	103	2	..	105	4	144
Me.	29	5	..	34(f)	2	80	70	1	151	2	185
Md.	22	7	..	29(g)	4	117	25	..	142(h)	4	171(h)
Mass.	27	13	..	40	2	169	69	1	240(d)	2	280(d)
Mich.	23	15	..	38	2(i)	73	37	..	110	2	148
Minn.	Nonpartisan election		..	67	4	Nonpartisan election		..	135	2	202
Miss.	52	..	..	52	4	122	..	..	122	4	174

Mo	23	11	..	..	34	4	124	39	..	163	2	197
Mont.	32	24	..	..	56(i)	4	56	38	..	94(i)	2	150(i)
Neo.	Nonpartisan election				49	4(k)	Unicameral legislature				..	49
Nev.	8	8	..	..	17(d,1)	4	25	12	..	37(l)	2	54(d)
N.H.	8	16	..	..	24	2	177	220	3	400(m)	2	424(m)
N.J.	6	15	..	..	21(n)	4(o)	28	32	..	60	2(o)	81(n)
N.M.	28	4	..	..	32(p)	4	59	18	..	77(p)	2	98(p)
N.Y.	33	25	..	..	58	2	88	62	1	151	2	209
N.C.	49	1	..	..	50	2	106	14	..	120	2	170
N.D.	20	29	..	..	49	4	65	44	..	109	2	158
Ohio	16	16	..	..	32(q)	4(q)	62	75	..	137(q)	2(q)	169(q)
Okla. (r)	41	7	..	..	48	4	78	21	..	99	2	147

(a) After November 8, 1966, 177 House members by 1965 reapportionment.

(b) Includes one holdover Democrat whose term expires November, 1966.

(c) Provided by statute enacted February, 1963, after constitutional provisions were declared invalid.

(d) The following numbers of members in current legislatures are not designated as Democrats or Republicans: Georgia Senate, 1; Massachusetts House, 1; Nevada Senate, 1; South Dakota Senate, 1; Vermont House, 5.

(e) The Illinois Supreme Court on July 29, 1965, ordered all State Senators to run for reelection in 1966. Unless a constitutionally valid reapportionment plan is passed by the legislature, Senators will be required to run for reelection again in 1968.

(f) Constitutional total of Senate members may vary according to population.

(g) To increase to 43 in election of 1966.

(h) For term of office ending in 1966 only, House members fixed at 142; thereafter House members revert to 123.

(i) Beginning with 1966 elections, Senate term four years.

(j) By federal court order on August 6, 1965, both houses of Montana legislature were reapportioned. All members of 1967 Legislative Assembly elected under a court-ordered plan at general election in November, 1966 (55 Senators and 104 Representatives).

(k) In 1966 all legislators elected for four years.

(l) Total number of legislators cannot exceed 75; number of Senators cannot be less than $1/3$ nor more than $1/2$ the number of Assemblymen.

(m) Constitutional total of House members cannot be less than 375 nor more than 400.

(n) Reapportionment accomplished in 1965 for November general election increased Senate to 29.

(o) All members of Senate and House stood for reelection in November, 1965, under a temporary reapportionment plan.

(p) By act of 1965 session, Senate membership set at 37 and House at 70. Senate reapportionment pending.

(q) At the reapportionment following the decennial census, a ratio is established to provide for fractional representation during the succeeding decade. Any county or senatorial district with a population larger than the minimum requirement for a Representative or Senator is allotted fractional additional representation by adding a Representative or Senator for one to four of the legislative sessions during the decade.

(r) As reapportioned by the U.S. District Court for the Western District of Oklahoma.

TABLE 4–2 (Cont.) **THE LEGISLATORS** · Numbers, Terms and Party Affiliations (as of August 1, 1965)

State or other jurisdiction	Senate					House					Constitutional total of legislators
	Dem	Rep	Vacancies	Constitutional total	Term	Dem	Rep	Vacancies	Constitutional total	Term	
Ore.	19	11	..	30	4	28	32	..	60	2	90
Pa.	22	27	1	50	4	116	93	..	209	2	259
R. I.	30	16	..	46	2	76	24	..	100	2	146
S. C.	46	..	..	46	4	123	1	..	124	2	170
S. D.	16	18	..	35(d)	2	30	45	..	75	2	110(d)
Tenn.	24	7	2	33	2	75	24	..	99	2	132
Tex.	31	..	..	31	4	149	1	..	150	2	181
Utah	15	12	..	27(s)	4	39	30	..	69	2	96(s)
Vt.	12	18	..	30	2	64	177	..	246(d,t)	2	276(d)
Va.	37	3	..	40	4	89	11	..	100	2	140
Wash.	32	17	..	49	4	60	39	..	99	2	148
W. V.	27	7	..	34	4	91	9	..	100	2	134
Wis.	13	20	..	33(u)	4	52	48	..	100(u)	2	133(u)
Wyo.	12	13	..	25	4	31	27	3	61	2	86
P. R.	23(v)	9(w)	..	32	4	47(v)	17(w)	..	64	4	96(x)

(s) After election of November 6, 1966, Senate membership will increase to 29.

(t) Following a special election in November, 1965, the reapportioned Vermont House was to have 150 members.

(u) Constitution sets number of Assemblymen at not less than 54 nor more than 100; number of Senators not less than $1/4$ nor more than $1/3$ the number of Assemblymen.

(v) Popular Democratic Party.

(w) Statehood Republican Party.

(x) The Puerto Rico constitution provides for selection of additional members from minority parties after each general election. Such selection is based fundamentally on the number of votes received by each minority party.

Source: *Frank Smothers, ed., The Book of the States: 1966–67 (Chicago: The Council of State Governments, 1966), p. 45.*

electing their own leaders. In states with partisan competition, the majority caucus may select the presiding officers. There may be intense competition for these positions, especially if the presiding officer assigns members to committees; in this case, candidates for the position of speaker use promises of committee assignments as their trading stock in soliciting support.

Formal leaders are most likely to be powerful if they are the actual spokesmen for their parties in a legislature with a high degree of party competition and party cohesion. In such legislatures the caucus may assume considerable importance as a decision-making institution. In Connecticut and New Jersey, critical decisions on determining legislative programs are made in caucus and then simply ratified by the majority members on the floor. In these circumstances, party leaders are the effective leaders of the legislature; and in some states the state party chairman, although not a legislator, meets with the legislators in caucus.

Even in the "nonpartisan" Minnesota legislature, caucuses are an important institution: a liberal caucus and a conservative caucus in each house assume all the characteristics of party caucuses in other states.[1]

COMMITTEES

In state legislatures, committees are not the powerful, independent, decision-making institutions that they are in Congress;[2] but they influence some decisions, and it is customary to refer amost all bills to them after the bill has been introduced.

Although the median number of state legislative committees has been declining, they are usually too numerous to operate effectively. The median number of senate and lower-house committees is now approximately 20; however, as Table 4–3 indicates, Mississippi has 50 committees in the house and 46 in the senate. The proliferation of committees enables most members to appear impressive by being able to list a committee chairmanship on a letterhead, but it does not necessarily contribute to effective lawmaking. Most studies indicate, moreover,

[1]G. Theodore Mitau, *Politics in Minnesota* (Minneapolis: University of Minnesota Press, 1960), Chap. 3, "A Nonpartisan Partisan Legislature," pp. 57–79; and Ralph S. Fjelstad, "How About Party Labels?" *National Municipal Review*, XLIV (July, 1955), 359–64.

[2]The literature on committees is naturally more extensive for the national Congress than for state legislatures. Some general treatments which take account of state as well as national committees are: Malcolm E. Jewell and Samuel C. Patterson, *The Legislative Process in the United States* (New York: Random House, 1966), Chap. 18; William J. Keefe and Morris S. Ogul, *The American Legislative Process: Congress and the States* (Englewood Cliffs, N.J.: Prentice-Hall, Inc., 1964), chap. 5 and 6; and George S. Blair, *American Legislatures: Structure and Process* (New York: Harper & Row, Publishers, 1967), Chap. 8. For useful studies of state committee systems, see: Wayne L. Francis, "Influence and Interaction in a State Legislative Body," *American Political Science Review*, LVI (December, 1962), 953–60; and Loren P. Beth and William C. Havard, "Committee Stacking and Political Power in Florida," *Journal of Politics*, XXIII (February, 1961), 57–83.

TABLE 4–3

LEGISLATIVE PROCEDURE: STANDING COMMITTEES AND HEARINGS

State or other jurisdiction	House committees appointed by Speaker	Senate committees appointed by	No. of standing committees at 1964 and 1965 regular sessions			Range in size of committees			Hearings open to public*
			House	Senate	Joint	House	Senate	Joint	
Ala.	★	President	19	30	0	7–15	3–21	.....	Dis.
Alaska	(a)	(a)	9	9(b)	0	7–11	5–7	.....	Dis.
Ariz.	★	President	21	21	0	11–15	7–14	.....	Dis.
Ark.	★	President	26	25	1	5–21	5–13	12	Dis.
Calif.	★★	Comm. on Rules	26	21	4	3–20	5–13	6–14	Yes
Colo.	★★	Resolution	16(c)	20	1	4–19	5–15	6	Dis.
Conn.	★(d)	Pres. pro tem(d)	0	0	28	.....	.....	27–41	Yes
Del.	★	Pres. pro tem	26	22	1	5	5	10	Dis.
Fla.	★★	President	49	44	0	5–23	7–19	.....	Yes(e)
Ga.	★★	President	24	19	0	5–51	3–22	.....	Dis.
Hawaii	★★	President	23(f)	19	0	3–17	2–10	.....	Dis.
Idaho	★★	President	15	14	0	7–17	5–11	.....	Dis.
Ill.	★★	Comm. on Comms.	23	24	0	6–35	3–22	.....	Yes
Ind.	★★	President	29	29	0	7–16	5–11	.....	Dis.
Iowa	★★	President	15	15	0	6–45	3–30	.....	Yes
Kan.	★★	Comm. on Comms.	45	31	1	3–23	5–13	12	Dis.
Ky.	(g)	President	44	19	0	4–45	9–22	.....	Dis.
La.	★★	President	18	19	0	9–20	3–17	.....	Dis.
Me.	★★	President	6	3	25	4–7	4–12	7–10	Yes
Md.	★★	President	15	16	3	6–31	3–15	6–10	Yes
Mass.	★★	President	6	4	31	3–16	3–10	15–19	Yes
Mich.	★★	Comm. on Comms.	41(h)	20(i)	1(j)	5–16(k)	6–9(l)	6(m)	Dis.
Minn.	★★	Comm. on Comms.	33	22	0	4–29	7–27	.....	Yes
Miss.	★	President	50	46	5	5–33	3–26	5–13	Dis.

State		Appointing authority							Dis.
Mo.		Pres. pro tem	47	30	3	5–50	5–15	15	Dis.
Mont.	★★	Comm. on Comms.	18	23	0	5–17	3–11	.....	Dis.
Neb.	(n)	Comm. on Comms.	(n)	14	(n)	(n)	1–9	(n)	Yes
Nev.	★★	President	21	19	0	5–9	3–5	.....	Yes
N. H.	★★	President	24	16	1	5–23	3–7	8	Yes
N. J.	★★	President	13	12	6	7–8	6–9	12	Dis.
N. M.	★★(o)	Comm. on Comms.	16(p)	7(q)	0	7–14	7–11	.....	Dis.
N. Y.	★★	Pres. pro tem	36	28	0	5–20	6–25	.....	Dis.
N. C.	★★★	President	46	34	1	12–61	7–25	21	Yes
N. D.	★★★	Comm. on Comms.	14	11	0	22	10–19	.....	Dis.
Ohio	★★★	Pres. pro tem	21	13	0	7–25	7–9	.....	Yes
Okla.	★★	(r)	36	36	0	3–31	3–28	.....	Dis.

*Abbreviation: Dis. — Discretionary.

(a) Nominated by Committee on Committees and elected by House and Senate respectively.
(b) Ten during 1964 session; 9 during 1965 session.
(c) Seventeen in 1964 session; 16 in 1965 session.
(d) Minority party members are nominated by the minority party leader of each house.
(e) Senate committees sometimes meet in executive session.
(f) Twenty-one in 1964 session; 23 in 1965 session.
(g) Committee on Committees.
(h) Forty-eight in 1964 session; 41 in 1965 session.
(i) Twenty-one in 1964 session; 20 in 1965 session.
(j) None in 1964 session; 1 in 1965 session.
(k) Five—fifteen in 1964 session; 5–16 in 1965 session.
(l) Six—ten in 1964 session; 6–9 in 1965 session.
(m) Six in 1965 session; no joint committee in 1964 session.
(n) Unicameral legislature.
(o) Standing Committee on Committees advises him.
(p) Only 12 consider legislation; 4 are procedural.
(q) Also the Committee on Committees.
(r) Senate elects Senate standing committees. Appointments to temporary and special committees are made by the Senate presiding officer.

TABLE 4–3 (Cont.) LEGISLATIVE PROCEDURE: STANDING COMMITTEES AND HEARINGS

State or other jurisdiction	House committees appointed by Speaker	Senate committees appointed by	No. of standing committees at 1964 and 1965 regular sessions			Range in size of committees			Hearings open to public*
			House	Senate	Joint	House	Senate	Joint	
Ore.	★	President	16	20	1	9	5–9	14	Yes
Pa.	★	Pres. pro tem	35	21	0	19	10–24	.....	Dis.
R. I.	★	Named in rules	15	17	1	9–17	5–13	9	Dis.
S. C.	★	Elected(s)	8	25	5	5–27	5–18	6–15	Dis.
S. D.	★	President	25(t)	16	0	3–15	3–9	.....	Dis.
Tenn.	★	Speaker	17	17	0	17–30	9–17	.....	Dis.
Tex.	★	President	43	24	1	5–21	5–21	6	Yes
Utah	★	President	16	14	1	7–19	3–13	32	Yes
Vt.	★	Special Comm.	18	18	3(u)	15	5–6	6	Yes
Va.	★	Elected	34	21	1	3–18	2–16	2	Dis.(v)
Wash.	★	President	24	20	0	9–47	6–31	.....	Dis.
W. V.	★	President	24	28	4	12–25	5–18	10–14	Yes
Wis.	★	Comm. on Comms.(w)	23	14	5	3–11	3–13	5–14	Yes
Wyo.	★	President	18	16	1	7–9	2–5	5	Dis.
P. R.	★	President	11	17	6	3–27	5–17	7–16	Dis.

(s) Special committees are appointed.
(t) Twenty-three in 1964 session; 25 in 1965 session.
(u) Corresponding committees of each house usually meet jointly.
(v) Final vote by a House committee must be held in open session.
(w) Confirmation by Senate.

Source: *Frank Smothers, ed., The Book of the States: 1966–67 (Chicago: The Council of State Governments, 1966), p. 53.*

that a few committees receive most of the bills, while other committees may seldom or never meet. In no state is the work load of committees evenly distributed. Rather, it is customary to assign the greatest number of bills to a small number of committees composed of members loyal to the leadership.

Most states have no clear-cut jurisdiction for committees. Unlike Congress, where the Legislative Reorganization Act of 1946 attempted to spell out jurisdictional lines among committees, most state legislatures simply designate committees by names and allow presiding officers to use discretion in assigning bills. Presiding officers in 35 state senates and 42 lower houses have discretion in the assignment of bills. It is common to have one or more committees designated "State Affairs," for example, to which any bill can be submitted. The fate of a bill may be determined by the committee to which it is sent. A bill adverse to the interest of farmers may be reported favorably by a commerce committee and never acted upon by an agriculture committee composed of farmers.

The assignment of members to committees and to committee chairmanships is as important as the assignment of bills to committees. Committee membership and chairmanship in the states are not so firmly based on seniority as they are in Congress, and the high turnover of state legislators does not permit the development of *expertise* that congressmen acquire from serving many years on the same committees.

Formally, the speaker of the lower house names members to committees and to chairmanships in forty-four states. In many of them, it is a tradition that the speaker in fact makes the critical decisions. Although restricted by some formal or informal factors such as geographic, factional, or party considerations, he may exercise wide discretion. Seniority is not often a determining factor in the selection of chairmen, nor does a member necessarily have the right to remain on a committee from one session to another. Because state legislatures do not usually require that minority representation on committees be proportional to membership in the house, it is common to fill important committees with majority members and to assign minority members to minor committees.[3] Even majority members who voted for the losing candidate for speaker may be discriminated against in committee assignments.

Formally, the presiding officer appoints members and chairmen to committees in thirty-three state senates, but there are significant differences between senates and lower houses in the amount of discretion involved in a formal appointment. If a lieutenant governor, who is not a member of the body, makes the formal appointments, he is less likely to be able to exercise his own personal discretion in selecting chairmen. In fact, there have been circumstances in which senates have entirely

[3]Beth and Havard, *op. cit.*, provide an interesting case study of this phenomenon in the Florida Legislature.

deprived lieutenant governors of the power to make appointments. Committees on committees play an important role in choosing committee members and chairmen in the other seventeen states. In general, since most state senators serve four-year terms through at least two sessions, seniority is given more consideration in state senates than in lower houses, but it is not the sole determining factor that it is in Congress.

To the extent that members' preferences are honored in selecting members, committees are not reflections of the total legislative body. Committees are generally composed of persons with occupational interests in the fields within their jurisdiction. It is customary to compose the judiciary committee with lawyers, the agriculture committee with farmers, the insurance committee with insurance agents, and so on. Whatever competence committees may have often derives from the members' occupational backgrounds, but to have those persons most immediately affected by proposed legislation assume primary responsibility for decisions may make it difficult, if not impossible, to pass legislation adverse to their interests. In those legislatures in which committees are an independent source of decision making, they are veto groups. A bill opposed by such committees may not pass; but since others know that the committee is stacked in favor of an interest, a bill promoted by the committee will be viewed with suspicion by others.

In many state legislatures, however, committee decisions are not conclusive. Some committees approve almost everything presented to them and thus throw the responsibility for actual decisions to the total membership. Formal rules also affect the relative power of committees. Both houses in fifteen states and one house in two other states require that committees report out all bills. On the other hand, both houses in three states and one house in seven other states have no method of forcing a bill from a committee.

Just as committees are weaker in state legislatures than they are in Congress, hearings of committees are much less important in the states than in Washington. Hearings *must* be held in public in twenty states, and they *may* be held in public in all states. Whether or not they are held at all makes relatively little difference, since they attract less attention than congressional hearings and are not often used as a device for eliciting facts. Often their more important function is simply to allow affected groups to present their views, with some notion that, whatever the result, the procedure will help reconcile the public to the results of legislative decision making. Table 4–3, cited before, lists those states in which hearings are required and those in which hearings are discretionary.

In addition to standing committees of each house, most states have some joint committees composed of members of both houses. Connecticut, Massachusetts, and Maine use joint committees predominantly for consideration of bills. State legislatures also use conference committees, composed on an *ad hoc* basis, to reconcile differences between bills passed in different forms in each house. States may also establish investigating committees. A few concerning subversive activities have even attracted considerable publicity, but no state legislature uses investigating committees as extensively as Congress does.

STAFF SERVICES

Where the legislature itself fails to provide adequate staff assistance, it becomes susceptible to outside influences. If the legislature is completely dependent on the executive for information and for bill drafting, the influence of the executive is increased. Or if members of the legislature are dependent on interest groups for assistance, the helpful groups have an influence denied to others.

Assistance for legislators began with legislative reference services in New York and Massachusetts at the turn of the century. In 1901, Wisconsin established a research agency to do "spot" research and bill drafting for legislators. It has been a model for many states.

In most states, now, legislative councils do more thorough research. Since the first legislative council was established in Kansas in 1933, forty-three states have adopted some form of this institution. New York and other states without a legislative council make extensive use of interim committees with professional staffs. Legislative councils are joint committees composed exclusively of legislators (although four states add other members) who meet between sessions to direct research and to report to the legislature. Two-thirds of the states authorize legislative councils to recommend bills to the legislature.

Legislative reference agencies and legislative councils are staffed with professional persons who can assist legislators. In most states, these agencies provide the principal staff available to legislators. Gradually, however, state legislatures are beginning to acquire staffs of their own. Improvement of staff services is one of the major concerns of the State Legislative Leaders Conference under the leadership of California's Assembly Speaker Jesse Unruh, whose own state has been in the forefront of the movement to give professional assistance to individual legislators and legislative committees. With Ford Foundation aid, fourteen states have instituted one-year internships of legislative service for young persons in law, journalism, and political science. As states begin acquiring staff assistants for committees, they usually add them first to committees on finance, judiciary, and appropriations.

Professional help is needed not only to produce legislation but also to clarify the legislative product. Almost all states now employ attorneys who specialize in statutory revision, a highly technical field concerned with eliminating archaic provisions in statutes and making certain that old conflicting sections of statutes are removed when new legislation is enacted.

Table 4–4 lists staff assistance now available in the states. The trend is clearly in the direction of more professional help for state legislators, although advocates of strengthened legislatures are far from satisfied. Some problems of staffing expert assistance are further discussed in Chapter VI, where proposals for reform are treated in greater detail.

TABLE 4–4

PERMANENT LEGISLATIVE SERVICE AGENCIES

State or other jurisdiction	Date agency established	Service agency	Reference library facilities	Bill drafting for legislature	Statutory revision	Legal counseling for legislators	Prepares bill and law summaries	Recommends substantive legislative program	Prepares research reports	Spot research	Continuous study of state revenues and expenditures	Budgetary review and analysis	Legislative post audit
Ala.	1945	Legislative Council	★	—	—	—	—	★	—	—	—	—	—
	1945	Legislative Reference Service*	★	★	★	★	★	—	★	★	—	—	—
	1947	Legislative Committee on Public Accounts	—	—	—	★	—	—	—	—	—	—	★
	1947	Dept. of Examiners of Public Accounts†	—	—	—	★	—	—	—	—	—	—	★
Alaska	1953	Legislative Council	★	★	★	★	★	★	★	★	★	★	—
	1955	Legislative Audit Committee	—	—	—	—	—	—	—	—	—	—	★
	1955	Division of Legislative Audit†	—	—	—	—	—	—	—	—	—	—	★
Ariz.	1953	Legislative Council	★	★	★	—	—	★	★	★	—	—	—
	1937	Dept. of Library and Archives	★	—	—	—	—	—	—	—	—	—	—
	1950	Post Auditor	—	—	—	—	—	—	—	—	—	—	★
Ark.	1947	Legislative Council	★	★	—	★	—	★	★	★	★	★(a)	—
	1947	Bureau of Legislative Research*	★	★	—	—	—	—	★	★	★	★(a)	—
	1953	Legislative Joint Auditing Committee	—	—	—	—	—	—	—	—	—	—	★
Calif.	1953	Division of Legislative Audit†	—	—	—	—	—	—	—	—	—	—	★
	1913	Legislative Counsel Bureau	—	★	★	★	★	—	★	★	—	—	★
	1904(b)	Administrative-Legislative Reference Service (State Library)	★	—	—	—	—	—	—	★	—	—	—
	1941	Joint Legislative Budget Committee	★	—	—	—	—	★	★	★	★	★	—
	1953	Law Revision Commission	—	—	★	—	—	★	—	—	—	—	—
	1955	Joint Legislative Audit Committee	—	—	—	—	—	—	—	—	—	—	★
	1955	Legislative Audit Bureau†	—	—	—	—	—	—	—	—	—	—	★
	1961	Legislative Reference Service (Assembly Committee on Rules)	★	—	—	—	—	—	★	★	—	—	—

State	Year	Agency																	
Colo.	1953	Legislative Council	★	—	—	—	★	—	—	—	—	—	—
	1927	Legislative Reference Office (Department of Law)	★	★	★	★	—	—	—	—	—	—	—
	1951	Committee on Statute Revision	★	—	—	—	—	—	—	—	—	—	—
	1956	Joint Budget Committee	—	—	—	—	—	—	—	★	★	—	—
	1965(c)	Legislative Audit Committee	—	—	★	★	★	—	—	—	—	—	—
Conn.	1937	Legislative Council	★	★	★	★	★	★	★	—	—	—	—
	1947	Legislative Research Department	★	★	★	★	★	★	★	—	—	—	—
	1907	Legislative Reference Section (State Library)	★	—	—	—	—	—	★	—	—	—	—
Del.	1902	Auditors of Public Accounts	★	★	★	★	★	★	—	—	—	—	—
	1945	Legislative Reference Bureau	★	★	★	★	★	★	★	—	—	—	—
Fla.	1949	Legislative Council	★	—	—	—	—	—	★	—	★	—	—
	1949	Legislative Reference Bureau*	★	★	★	★	★	—	—	★	—	★	—
	1939	Statutory Revision & Bill Drafting Depts. (Office of Attorney General)	—	—	—	—	—	—	—	—	—	—	—
	1955	Legislative Appropriations and Auditing Committee (Legislative Council)	—	—	—	—	★	—	★	★	★	—	—
Ga.	1959(d)	Legislative Services Committee	—	—	—	—	—	—	—	—	—	—	—

*Agency which provides staff services for legislative council or council-type agency, in eleven states.

†Agency which provides staff services for legislative fiscal review or audit committee, in seven states and Puerto Rico.

(a) Also responsible for preparing a state budget.

(b) Year legislative reference services were first provided within existing library agency.

(c) Colorado: Legislative Audit Committee created in 1965, to appoint State Auditor effective July 1, 1966, replacing elected State Auditor, which office goes out of existence January 1967; New Mexico: Legislative Audit Commission created in 1965, to appoint a Legislative Auditor, who will assume his duties January 1, 1967.

(d) Georgia: Joint Committee on Operations of the General Assembly created in 1959, replaced by Legislative Services Committee in 1961; Kentucky: Legislative Council created in 1936, replaced by Legislative Research Commission in 1948; Maryland: Department of Legislative Reference established as a department of the government of the city of Baltimore in 1907, functions expanded to include service to the state legislature in 1916, placed under jurisdiction of the legislative branch of state government in 1965; Minnesota: Legislative Research Committee established on a temporary basis in 1947, made permanent in 1951; North Carolina: Legislative Council created in 1963, replaced by Legislative Research Commission in 1965; Ohio: Program Commission created in 1943, replaced by Legislative Service Commission in 1953; Oklahoma: Legislative Council created in 1939, not activated until 1947; Rhode Island: Legislative Council created in 1939, not activated until 1959; Wisconsin: Legislative Reference Library created in 1901, name changed to Legislative Reference Bureau in 1963; Revisor of Statutes created in 1909, name changed to Statutory Revision Bureau in 1963; Wyoming: Legislative Research Committee created in 1959, replaced by Legislative Council in 1961, but inactive since 1963.

TABLE 4-4 (cont.)

PERMANENT LEGISLATIVE SERVICE AGENCIES

State or other jurisdiction	Date agency established	Service agency	Reference library facilities	Bill drafting for legislature	Statutory revision	Legal counseling for legislators	Prepares bill and law summaries	Recommends substantive legislative program	Prepares research reports	Spot research	Continuous study of state revenues and expenditures	Budgetary review and analysis	Legislative post audit
	1959	Office of Legislative Counsel*	★	★	★	★	★	—	★	★	—	—	—
	1914(b)	State Library	★	—	—	—	—	—	—	★★	—	—	—
	1923	Department of Audits and Accounts	—	—	—	—	—	—	—	★	—	—	★
Guam	1959	Information Office	★	—	—	—	★	—	★	★	—	—	—
	1950	Legislative Counsel to the Legislature	★	★	★	★	★	—	★	★	—	—	—
	1957	Legislative Auditor	—	—	—	—	—	—	—	—	—	—	★
Hawaii	1957	Legislative Fiscal Analyst	—	—	—	—	—	★★	★★	★★	★	★	—
	1943	Legislative Reference Bureau	★	★	—	★	★	—	★	★	—	—	—
	1959	Revisor of Statutes	—	—	★	—	—	—	—	—	—	—	—
	1959	Legislative Auditor	—	—	—	—	—	—	—	—	—	—	★
Idaho	1963	Legislative Council	★	★	★	★★	★	—	★★	★★	★	★	—
Ill.	1937	Legislative Council	—	—	—	★	—	—	★	★	—	—	—
	1913	Legislative Reference Bureau	★	★	★	★	★	—	—	★	—	★	—
	1937	Budgetary Commission	—	—	—	—	—	—	—	—	—	—	—
	1957	Legislative Audit Commission	—	—	—	—	—	—	—	★	★(e)	—	★(e)
Ind.	1945	Legislative Advisory Commission	★	★	—	—	★	★	★★	★	★	—	—
	1907	Legislative Bureau	—	★	★	—	—	—	★★	★	—	—	—
Iowa	1955	Legislative Research Committee	—	★	—	★	—	★	★	★★	—	—	—
	1955	Legislative Research Bureau*	★	—	—	—	—	—	★	★	—	—	—
	1939	Legislative Reference Bureau (State Law Library)	★	—	—	—	—	—	—	—	—	—	—
	1951	Budget & Financial Control Committee	—	—	—	—	—	—	—	—	★	★	—
	1961	Office of Legislative Fiscal Director†(f)	—	—	—	—	—	—	—	—	★	—	—
Kan.	1933	Legislative Council	★	—	—	—	—	★	★	★	—	—	—

Year	Agency												
1909(b)	State Library	★	—	—	—	—	—	—	—	—	—	—	—
1929	Revisor of Statutes	—	★	★	★	★	—	—	—	—	—	—	—
Ky. 1936(d)	Legislative Research Commission	★	★	★	★	★	★	★	—	—	—	—	—
La. 1952	Legislative Council	★	★	—	★	★	★	★	—	—	—	—	—
1946(b)	State Library	★	—	—	—	—	—	—	—	—	—	—	—
1938	State Law Institute	—	—	★	—	—	—	—	—	★	—	★	—
1962	Legislative Budget Committee	—	—	—	—	—	—	—	—	—	—	—	—
1962	Office of Legislative Auditor†	—	—	—	—	—	★	—	—	★	★	★	—
Me. 1939	Legislative Research Committee	★	★	★	★	★	★	★	★	★	—	★	—
....	Legislative Reference Section (State Library)	★	—	—	—	—	★	★	—	—	—	—	—
1907	Department of Audit	—	—	—	—	—	—	—	—	—	—	—	★
Md. 1939	Legislative Council	—	★	—	—	★	★	★	★	★	★	★	—
1916(d)	Department of Legislative Reference* (Dept. of Legislative Reference)	★	★	★	★	★	—	★	—	—	—	—	—
1947	Fiscal Research Bureau	★	—	—	—	—	—	★	—	★	★	★	—
....	State Library	★	—	—	—	—	—	—	—	—	—	—	—
Mass. 1954	Legislative Research Council	—	—	—	—	—	—	★	★	★	—	—	—
1954	Legislative Reference Bureau*	—	—	—	—	—	—	★	★	★	—	—	—
1908(b)	Legislative Reference Division (State Library)	★	—	—	—	—	—	—	★	★	—	—	—
....	Senate Counsel	—	★	★	★	★	—	—	★	★	—	—	—
....	House Counsel	—	★	★	★	★	—	—	★	★	—	★	—
1946(g)	House Ways and Means Committee	—	—	★	★	★	★	—	—	—	★	★	★
....	Senate Ways and Means Committee	—	—	—	—	—	—	★	—	★	★	★	—
Mich. 1965	Legislative Council	★	★	—	—	★	★	—	—	—	—	—	—
1941	Legislative Service Bureau*	★	★	★	★	★	★	★	—	★	—	—	—
1965	Law Revision Commission	—	—	—	—	—	★	—	—	—	—	—	—

(e) Illinois also created in 1957 the Department of Audits administered by an Auditor General appointed by the Governor and charged with post-audit duties. The Legislative Audit Commission sets policies for the Auditor General, conducts a post-audit of his office, and has broad power to make fiscal review studies for the legislature.

(f) Office temporarily discontinued July 1, 1965 by administrative order of the Budget and Financial Control Committee.

(g) Year in which full-time staff was organized.

TABLE 4–4 (cont.)

PERMANENT LEGISLATIVE SERVICE AGENCIES

State or other jurisdiction	Date agency established	Service agency	Reference library facilities	Bill drafting for legislature	Statutory revision	Legal counseling for legislators	Prepares bill and law summaries	Recommends substantive legislative program	Prepares research reports	Spot research	Continuous study of state revenues and expenditures	Budgetary review and analysis	Legislative post audit
	1965	Legislative Auditor General	—	—	—	—	—	—	—	—	—	—	★
	1965(g)	Senate Appropriations Committee	—	—	—	—	—	—	—	—	★	★	—
Minn.	1947(d)	Legislative Research Committee	★	—	—	—	—	—	—	—	—	—	—
	....	State Law Library	★	—	—	—	—	—	—	—	—	—	—
	1939	Revisor of Statutes	—	★	★	★	★	—	—	★	—	—	—
	1964(g)	Senate Finance Committee	—	—	—	—	—	—	—	★	★	★	—
	1965(g)	House Appropriations Committee	—	—	—	—	—	—	—	★	★	★	—
Miss.	....	State Library	★	—	—	—	—	—	—	—	—	—	—
	1944	Revisor of Statutes	—	★	★	★	—	—	—	★	—	—	—
	1955	Commission of Budgeting & Accounting (Dept. of Justice)	—	—	—	—	—	—	—	—	★	★	—
Mo.	1943	Committee on Legislative Research	★	★	★	—	—	—	★	★	—	—	—
	1965	Committee on State Fiscal Affairs	—	—	—	—	—	—	—	—	★	—	—
Mont.	1957	Legislative Council	★	★	★	★	—	★	★	★	★	★	—
Neb.	1937	Legislative Council	★	★	—	—	★	★	★	★	★	—	—
	1945	Revisor of Statutes	—	★	★	—	—	—	—	—	—	—	—
Nev.	1945	Legislative Commission	★	—	★	★	—	★	★	★	★	★	—
	1945	Legislative Counsel Bureau*	★	—	—	★	★	★	★	★	—	—	★
	....	State Library	★	—	—	—	—	—	—	—	—	—	—
N.H.	1951	Legislative Council	—	—	—	—	—	—	—	★	—	—	—
	1963	Director of Legislative Services	—	★	★	—	—	—	—	—	—	—	—

State	Year	Service
	1913(b)	Legislative Service (State Library)
	1947	Legislative Budget Assistant
N. J.	1957	Counsel to the Senate
	1954	Law Revision and Legislative Services Commission
	1954	Legislative Budget and Finance Director
	1945	Law and Legislative Reference Bureau (Division of the State Library)
	1933	Department of State Audit
N. M.	1951	Legislative Council
	1951	Legislative Council Service*
	1957	Legislative Finance Committee
	1965(c)	Legislative Audit Commission
N. Y.	....	Legis. Reference Library (State Library)
	1901	Legislative Bill Drafting Commission
	1934	Law Revision Commission
	1959	Office of Legislative Research(h)
N. C.	1963(d)	Legislative Research Commission
	1945	General Statutes Commission (Department of Justice)
	1939	Division of Legislative Drafting & Codification of Statutes (Department of Justice)
	1947	Revisor of Statutes (Department of Justice)
	....	State Library

(h) Established jointly by the Speaker of the House and the President Pro Tem of the Senate, and does research under their direction.

TABLE 4-4 (cont.)

PERMANENT LEGISLATIVE SERVICE AGENCIES

State or other jurisdiction	Date agency established	Service agency	Reference library facilities	Bill drafting for legislature	Statutory revision	Legal counseling for legislators	Prepares bill and law summaries	Recommends substantive legislative program	Prepares research reports	Spot research	Continuous study of state revenues and expenditures	Budgetary review and analysis	Legislative post audit
N. D.	1945	Legislative Research Committee	★	★	★	★	—	★	★	★	—	★	—
	1963	Committee on Audits and Fiscal Review	—	—	—	—	—	—	—	—	—	—	★
Ohio	1943(d)	Legislative Service Commission	★	★	★	★	★	★	★	★★★	★	★	—
	1910	Legislative Reference Bureau	★	★	—	★	★★	—	—	★★	—	—	—
Okla.	1939(d)	State Legislative Council	—	—	—	—	★★	★	★	★★	—	—	—
	1951	Legislative Audit Committee (Legislative Council)	—	—	—	—	—	—	—	—	★	★	★★
	1965	Division of Bill Drafting & Statutory Revision (Legislative Council)	—	★	★	—	—	—	—	—	—	—	—
	1917(i)	Legislative Reference and Research Division (State Library)	★	—	—	—	★	—	★	★	—	—	—
Ore.	1953	Legislative Counsel Committee	—	★	★	★	★	★	★	★★★	—	—	—
	1913(b)	State Library	★	—	—	—	—	—	—	★★★	—	—	—
Pa.	1959	Legislative Fiscal Committee	—	—	—	—	—	★★	★★	★★	★	★	—
	1937	Joint State Government Commission	★	—	—	—	—	—	—	—	★	—	—
	1909	Legislative Reference Bureau	★	★	—	★	★	—	—	—	—	—	—
	1959	Legislative Budget and Finance Committee	—	—	—	—	—	—	★	★★	★	★	—
	.....	Senate Appropriations Committee	★	—	—	—	—	—	—	★★	—	★★	★★
	.....	House Appropriations Committee	★	—	—	—	—	—	—	★★	—	★★	★★

State	Year	Service
P. R.	1954	Office of Legislative Services
	1950	Commission for the Codification of the Laws
	1954	Joint Legislative Committee on Reports from the Controller
	1952	Office of Controller†
R. I.	1939(d)	Legislative Council
	1907(b)	Legislative Reference Bureau (State Library)
	....	Assistant in Charge of Law Revision (Office of Secretary of State)
	1939	Finance Committee of House of Representatives
S. C	1949	Legislative Council
	1954	Code Commissioner
S. D.	1951	Legislative Research Council
	1951	Revisor of Statutes
	1943	Department of Audits and Accounts
Tenn.	1953	Legislative Council Committee
	....	State Library and Archives
	1953	Code Commission
	1835	Department of Audit
Tex.	1949	Legislative Council
	1909	Legislative Reference Division (State Library)
Utah	1949	Legislative Budget Board
	1943	Legislative Audit Committee
	1947	Legislative Council
	....	State Library
Vt.	1965	Legislative Council
	1957	Statutory Revision Commission

(i) Services established in 1917; division formalized by statute in 1949.

TABLE 4–4 (cont.)

PERMANENT LEGISLATIVE AGENCIES

State or other jurisdiction	Date agency established	Service agency	Reference library facilities	Bill drafting for legislature	Statutory revision	Legal counseling for legislators	Prepares bill and law summaries	Recommends substantive legislative program	Prepares research reports	Spot research	Continuous study of state revenues and expenditures	Budgetary review and analysis	Legislative post audit
Va.	1936	Advisory Legislative Council	★	—	—	—	—	★	★	—	—	—	—
	1914	Division of Statutory Research and Drafting*	—	★	★	★	★	—	★	★	—	—	—
	1948	Code Commission	—	—	★	★	—	—	—	—	—	—	—
	1928	General Assembly Auditing Committee	—	—	—	—	—	—	—	—	—	—	★
	1928	Auditor of Public Accounts†	—	—	—	—	—	—	—	—	—	—	★
V. I.	....	Legislative Consultant	—	★	—	—	—	—	★	★	—	—	—
Wash.	1947	State Legislative Council	—	★	—	★	★	★	★	★	—	—	—
	....	State Library	★	—	—	—	—	—	—	★	—	—	—
	1951	Legislative Budget Committee	—	—	—	—	—	—	—	—	★	★	—
	1951	Statute Law Committee	—	★	★	★	—	—	★	—	—	—	—
W. Va.	1947	Joint Committee on Government and Finance(i)	—	—	—	—	—	—	★	—	★	★	★
	1953	Legislative Auditor (Joint Committee on Government and Finance)	★	—	—	—	—	—	—	—	—	—	—
	1965	Legislative Services (Joint Committee on Government and Finance)	—	★	★	★	—	★	★	★	—	—	—
Wis.	1947	Joint Legislative Council	—	—	—	—	★	★	★	—	—	—	—
	1901(d)	Legislative Reference Bureau	★	★	—	—	★	—	★	★	—	—	—
	1909(d)	Statutory Revision Bureau	—	—	★	—	—	—	—	—	—	—	—
Wyo.	1959(d)	Legislative Council	★	—	—	—	—	—	—	★	—	—	—
	....	State Library	★	—	—	—	—	—	—	—	—	—	—
	1959	Statutes Revision Commission	—	—	★	—	—	—	—	—	—	—	—

(i) Carries on interim research program in conjunction with Commission on Interstate Cooperation.

From Frank Smothers, ed., The Book of the States: 1966–67 (Chicago: The Council of State Governments, 1966), pp. 74–78.

SESSIONS

Annual sessions of legislatures were common until the late nineteenth century, when distrust of legislatures resulted in increasing restrictions on their sessions. At the end of World War II, only four states had annual sessions; all other states had biennial sessions. Now the trend is in the other direction: twenty states have annual sessions; thirty states have biennial sessions. Half the states holding annual sessions deal with only the budget during the off-year session.

State constitutions restrict the length of sessions in most states. Seventeen states have no restrictions on length of regular sessions, but some cut them down to 30 calendar days.

Special sessions during the last decade were called by the dozen but avoided by only the half-dozen. In most states, the governor decides whether or not to call a special session; and in all but six states, they were called. A dozen states permit legislative initiative in calling special sessions; but a dozen governors specify the subject that is to be considered, and only that matter may be taken up.

In spite of these restrictions, sessions are getting longer all the time — particularly special sessions.

In Massachusetts, Wisconsin, and other states without restrictions on sessions, legislatures have recessed — instead of adjourning — sine die, so that they could continue meeting as the need arose throughout the term. This procedure is a variant of the "split session," a system under which the legislature meets for the introduction of bills, recesses while the committees deliberate on them, and then reconvenes only to consider the bills introduced earlier.

PROCEDURAL RULES

The first and most important procedural rules for state legislatures allot time in which they can meet. The length of sessions is a factor in determining how carefully they may consider proposals placed before them and how many issues can be considered. A legislature rushing to adjourn is a scene of utter confusion: roll call quickly follows roll call, to the point that members may have little notion of what they are deciding.

In formal terms, bills may be introduced only by legislators or special legislative bodies such as the legislative council or legislative committees. It is even common to refer to the legislator who introduces a bill as the "author," but actually very few proposals emanate from the legislators themselves. The initiative for most proposals comes from the governor and other executives, interest groups, and sometimes a constituent. Legislators may feel that there ought to be a law, but they know that one now needs a legal expert to draft it. This service was formerly often performed by the attorney general's office, but legislatures are now generally establishing their own bill drafting services.

When a proposal has been drafted, it may be formally introduced by

TABLE 4—5

LEGISLATIVE SESSIONS

State or other jurisdiction	Years in which sessions are held	Sessions convene		Limitations on length of sessions		Special sessions	
		Month	Day	Regular	Special	Legislature may call	Legislature may determine subject
Ala.	Odd	May	1st Tues.(a)	36 L	36 L	No	2/3 vote those present
Alaska	Annual	Jan.	4th Mon.	None	30 C	Yes	Yes(b)
Ariz.	Annual	Jan.	2nd Mon.	63 C(c)	20 C(c)	Petition 2/3 members	Yes(d)
Ark.	Odd	Jan.	2nd Mon.	60 C	15 C(e)	No	(e)
Calif.	Annual(f)	Jan.	Odd-Mon. after Jan. 1	120 C(g)	None	No	No
		Feb.	Even-1st Mon.	30 C			
Colo.	Annual(f)	Jan.	Wed. after 1st Tues.	160 C(c)	None	No	No
Conn.	Odd	Jan.	Wed. after 1st Mon.	150 C(h)	None	Yes	Yes
Del.	Annual(f)	Jan.	Odd-1st Tues.	90 L	30(c)	No	Yes
		Feb.	Even-1st Tues.	30 L			
Fla.	Odd	Apr.	Tues. after 1st Mon.	60 C(i)	20 C(i)	(i)	Yes(j)
Ga.	Annual	Jan.	Odd-2nd Mon.	45 C(k)	(l)	Petition 3/5 members(m)	Yes(d)
		Jan.	Even-2nd Mon.	40 C			
Hawaii	Annual(f)	Feb.	Odd-3rd Wed.	60 C(n)	30 C(n)	(o)	(o)
		Feb.	Even-3rd Wed.	30 C(n)			
Idaho	Odd	Jan.	Mon. after Jan. 1	60 C(c)	20 C	No	No
Ill.	Odd	Jan.	Wed. after 1st Mon.	None(p)	None	No	No
Ind.	Odd	Jan.	Thurs. after 1st Mon.	61 C	40 C	No	Yes
Iowa	Odd	Jan.	2nd Mon.	None	None	No	Yes(q)
Kan.	Annual(f)	Jan.	Odd-2nd Tues.	90 L(c)	30 L(c)	No	Yes
		Jan.	Even-2nd Tues.	30 C			
Ky.	Even	Jan.	Tues. after 1st Mon.	60 L	None	No	No
La.	Annual(f)	May	Even-2nd Mon.	60 C	None	Petition 2/3 elected members each house	No(r)
		May	Odd-2nd Mon.	30 C	30 C		
Me.	Odd	Jan.	1st Wed.	None	None	No	Yes
Md.	Annual	Jan.	3rd Wed.	70 C	30 C	No	Yes
Mass.	Annual	Jan.	1st Wed.	None	None	Yes	Yes
Mich.	Annual	Jan.	2nd Wed.	None	None	No	No
Minn.	Odd	Jan.	Tues. after 1st Mon.	120 L	None	No	Yes
Miss.	Even	Jan.	Tues. after 1st Mon.	None	None	No	No
Mo.	Odd	Jan.	Wed. after Jan. 1	195 C(h)	60 C	No	No

Mont.	Odd	Jan.	1st Mon.	60 C	60 C	No	No
Neb.	Odd	Jan.	1st Tues.	None	None	Petition 2/3 members	No
Nev.	Odd	Jan.	3rd Mon.	60 C(c)	20 C(c)	No	No
N. H.	Odd	Jan.	1st Wed.	July 1(c)	15 L(c)	Yes	Yes
N. J.	Annual	Jan.	2nd Tues.	None	None	(s)	Yes
N. M.	Annual(f)	Jan.	Odd-3rd Tues.	60 C	30 C(t)	Yes(t)	Yes(t)
		Jan.	Even-3rd Tues.	30 C			

Abbreviations: L—Legislative days; C—Calendar days

(a) Legislature meets quadrennially on second Tuesday in January after election for purpose of organizing.

(b) Unless Governor calls and limits.

(c) Indirect restriction on session length. Legislators' pay, per diem, or daily allowance ceases but session may continue. In Colorado the 160-day limitation applies to the legislative biennium. In New Hampshire travel allowance ceases after July 1 or 90 legislative days, whichever occurs first.

(d) If legislature convenes itself.

(e) Governor may convene General Assembly for specified purpose. After specific business is transacted, a $2/3$ vote of members of both houses may extend sessions up to 15 days.

(f) Budget sessions held in even-numbered years, except in Louisiana.

(g) Exclusive of Saturdays and Sundays.

(h) Approximate length of session. Connecticut session must adjourn by first Wednesday after first Monday in June, Missouri's by July 15, and Puerto Rico's by April 30.

(i) Length of session may be extended by 30 days, but not beyond Sept. 1, by $3/5$ vote of both houses.

(j) Twenty per cent of the membership may petition the Secretary of State to poll the legislature; upon affirmative vote of $3/5$ of both houses an extra session, no more than 30 days in length, may be called. Extra sessions called by the Governor are limited to 20 days.

(k) Convenes for no longer than 12 days to organize. Recesses and then reconvenes 2nd Monday in February for not more than 33 calendar days. Budget presently considered in odd-year session only.

(l) Seventy-day session limit except for impeachment proceedings if Governor calls session; 30-day limit except for impeachment proceedings if Governor calls session at petition of legislature.

(m) Thirty-day limit except for impeachment proceedings.

(n) Governor may extend any session for not more than 30 days. Sundays and holidays shall be excluded in computing the number of days of any session.

(o) Legislature may convene in special session on 45th day after adjournment to act on bills submitted to the Governor less than ten days before adjournment if Governor notifies the legislature he plans to return them with objections.

(p) By custom legislature adjourns by July 1, since all bills passed after that day are not effective until July 1 of following year.

(q) Iowa constitution requires the Governor to inform both houses of the General Assembly the purpose for which a special session has been convened.

(r) Unless legislature petitions for special session. However, no special session may be called during the 30 days before or the 30 days after the regular fiscal sessions in the odd years without the consent of $3/4$ of the elected members of each house of the legislature.

(s) Petition by majority of members of each house to Governor, who then "shall" call special session.

(t) Limitation does not apply if impeachment trial is pending or in process. Legislature may call 30-day "extraordinary" session if Governor refuses to call session when requested by $3/5$ of legislature.

TABLE 4—5 (Cont.)

LEGISLATIVE SESSIONS

State or other jurisdiction	Years in which sessions are held	Sessions convene		Limitations on length of sessions		Special sessions	
		Month	Day	Regular	Special	Legislature may call	Legislature may determine subject
N. Y.	Annual	Jan.	Wed. after 1st Mon.	None	None	No	No
N. C.	Odd	Feb.	Wed. after 1st Mon.	120 C(c)	25 C(c)	No	Yes
N. D.	Odd	Jan.	Tues. after 1st Mon.	60 L	None	No	Yes
Ohio	Odd	Jan.	1st Mon.	None	None	No	No
Okla.	Odd	Jan.	Tues. after 1st Mon.	None	None	No(u)	No
Ore.	Odd	Jan.	2nd Mon.	None	None	No	Yes
Pa.	Annual(f)	Jan.	1st Tues.	None	None	No	No
R. I.	Annual	Jan.	1st Tues.	60 L(c)	None	No	No
S. C.	Annual	Jan.	2nd Tues.	None	40 L(c)	No	Yes
S. D.	Annual(f)	Jan.	Odd-Tues. after 3rd Mon. / Even-Tues. after 1st Mon.	45 L / 30 L	None	No	Yes
Tenn.	Odd	Jan.	1st Mon.	75 C(c)	20 C(c)	No	No
Tex.	Odd	Jan.	2nd Tues.	140 C	30 C	No	No
Utah	Odd	Jan.	2nd Mon.	60 C	30 C	No	No
Vt.	Odd	Jan.	Wed. after 1st Mon.	None	None	No	Yes
Va.	Even	Jan.	2nd Wed.	60 C(c,v)	30 C(c,v)	Petition 2/3 members	Yes
Wash.	Odd	Jan.	2nd Mon.	60 C	None	No	Yes
W. Va.	Annual(f)	Jan.	Odd-2nd Wed. / Even-2nd Wed.	60 C(w) / 30 C(w)	None	Petition 2/3 members	No
Wis.	Odd	Jan.	2nd Wed.	None	None	No	No
Wyo.	Odd	Jan.	2nd Tues.	40 C	None	No	Yes
P. R.	Annual	Jan.	2nd Mon.	111 C(h,x)	20	No	No

(u) Governor may convene Senate alone in special session.
(v) May be extended up to 30 days by 3/5 vote of each house, but without pay.
(w) Must be extended by Governor until general appropriation passed; may be extended by 2/3 vote of legislature.
(x) Session may be extended by adoption of joint resolution.

From Frank Smothers, ed., The Book of the States: 1966—67 (Chicago: The Council of State Governments, 1966), pp. 46—47.

submitting it to the clerk during a specified time on the daily calendar. In many legislatures, bills can be introduced only at the beginning of the legislative session.

After the bill is introduced, it is given a series of "readings" (usually three) as it proceeds to committee and then is returned to the full house for deliberation. This terminology derives from the British Parliament, where, before literacy was common, a clerk read a bill three separate times, so that it would be understood. Even now, when literacy is common and printing presses are available to provide all members with copies of bills, it is customary to discuss legislative process in terms of "readings," although the reading usually consists of having a clerk read the number and title. After introduction and usually after "first reading," a bill is sent to committee. Here, as we have learned, its fate may be determined by the particular rules of a given legislative body. Some legislatures require committees to report all bills, some have no provision for forcing a bill from committee, and others do not require all bills to be reported but can force a bill from committee. Apart from these formal rules, traditions of committees vary, and some committees report out all bills although the rules may not require it.

After a bill is reported by a committee, it goes onto the calendar. Unlike the complications of the U.S. House of Representatives, with its four calendars and its powerful rules committee, most state legislatures have only one calendar and take up bills in the order in which they were reported.

There are two steps in the chamber's deliberation on the bill. During the first step, the bill is subject to amendment. Amendments are voted on first. After all amendments have been considered, a vote is taken on "engrossment," which is putting the bill in final form so that it is no longer subject to amendment. Later, after the passage of one or two legislative days, a vote is taken on final passage.

During the deliberation stage, members have an opportunity to "debate" on the floor. Except on minor matters or unanticipated amendments, however, speeches on the floor are not often a factor in persuading members how to vote. On important matters, they may have committed themselves long before the bill comes to the floor. On less important matters, there are many cue mechanisms—party, faction, friendship—other than the arguments on the merits of the bills. Because the newspapers give state legislatures less attention than they give Congress, there is less motivation for members to address themselves to the public. Unless a delegation of school children from a legislator's district is present in the gallery, there is little motive for oratory. Thus, "debate" may be restricted to statements meaningful to members only: "This don't do nothing to nobody." "This is an agreed bill." "This is purely correctional and is needed to plug a loophole in the X law."

There is no equivalent of the filibuster in state legislatures. All legislatures have means for terminating debate, and many of them have restrictions on the length of time that members may speak or prohibitions against any member's speaking more than once without special permission. More important than these rules, however, are often the norms of the body. While there is a great reluctance to keep persons from speaking, members also recognize that speaking too long or too often hurts their cause. Especially in those legislative bodies where electric voting machines are used, the members must remain in or near the legislative chamber. Unlike Congressmen, they cannot retire to their offices and then rush to the chamber to vote. As a result, they do not wish to be bored by long speeches, and the perceptive members understand that and limit their floor oratory accordingly.

Decisions in state legislatures are made by voice vote or roll calls. Voice votes are used for minor matters or procedural votes on which the result is not in doubt. Teller votes and divisions are not often used. Rather, many roll calls are conducted—far more than in Congress—in which the vote of each member is recorded. Some states require a roll call on final passage; but even where not required, a specified number of members may request a roll call. The taking of these votes is greatly facilitated in the thirty-five chambers that have electric voting machines.

Once a bill has passed in its house of origin, it is sent to the other house, where all the steps described here are repeated (except in Connecticut, Massachusetts, and Maine, where joint committees are used). If the bill passes the second house in the same form as it passed the first house, it is ready to be sent to the governor. If differing versions are passed in the two houses and each house adheres to its position, a conference committee composed of members of both houses is constituted on an *ad hoc* basis to work out a compromise. After the conference committee has reported, each chamber may either accept or reject its report; it cannot amend the conference report.

After the bill has passed both houses in the same form, it is sent to the governor, who has a veto in all states except North Carolina. The American governor has more power in the function of considering bills than the American President has. Most bills in state legislatures are passed at the end of a session, giving the governor more frequent opportunities than the President has for use of the pocket veto. With a pocket veto, the governor does not have to explain his action by sending a bill back to the legislature: it simply fails to become a law because he has not signed it. More important, forty-one governors have an item veto, which the President does not have, over appropriations measures. Governors may approve of parts of bills and reject other parts. In four states—Massachusetts, Alabama, Virginia, and New Jersey—the governor has even greater discretion: the power of executive amendment. He may return the bill with his own amendments, and the legislature must consider these amendments. Since most states require an extraordinary majority to override a veto, few measures are passed over it.

Although the formal rules of state legislatures vary from state to state and chamber to chamber, they are not anywhere as complex as in the United States Congress. Nor is it as common in state legislatures to use the technicalities of rules for strategic advantages. Presiding officers frequently assist members by instructing them in the motions they must make to achieve their purposes, or even the presiding officer may state requests properly when the novice member is not able to do so.

Moreover, the rules may often be bypassed. By unanimous consent, any rule can be set aside and business expedited. Especially during the rush to adjourn, many procedural steps are taken by unanimous consent to suspend rules. The normal processes described here take many days, but the use of consent calendars for noncontroversial bills or the granting of unanimous consent short-circuits these processes. When there is overwhelming support for a measure, such as a legislative pay raise, a bill can be introduced and rushed through both houses of a state legislature in a few hours.

Special procedures peculiar to each legislative chamber are also used to circumvent the usual rules. Some states use the "short roll call," in which clerks read merely the first and last name on the membership roster and report enough favorable votes to pass the bill. Courts have refused to look behind the validity of legislative journals when laws passed in this manner have been questioned. Similarly, some states use special procedures for local bills, which are passed in skeleton sessions attended by only the legislator from the county affected, but with a report of a quorum in the legislative journal. Such devices help to alleviate some of the problems created by cumbersome formal rules.

GROUP NORMS

Informal rules of state legislatures are as important as formal procedural rules. Like all human groups, legislatures have their own norms which new members are expected to learn and abide by and their own sanctions for those who violate rules.

Wahlke and his associates who interviewed legislators in California, New Jersey, Ohio, and Tennessee report that legislators listed forty-two "rules of the game"[4] and ranked these among the most important: performance of obligations (keeping your word); respect for other members' legislative rights; impersonality (oppose the bill, not the man); self-restraint in debate (don't talk too much); and courtesy.

The rules serve to:

1) promote group cohesion and solidarity
2) promote predictability of legislative behavior
3) channel and restrain conflict
4) expedite legislative business
5) give tactical advantages to individual members[5]

Legislators recognize that they have institutional interests apart from interests in others whom they represent, and they have developed

[4]John C. Wahlke, Heinz Eulau, William Buchanan, and LeRoy C. Ferguson, *The Legislative System: Explorations in Legislative Behavior* (New York: John Wiley & Sons, Inc., 1962), pp. 146–47.
[5]*Ibid.*, pp. 160–61.

norms promoting institutional patriotism. But Jewell and Patterson maintain that institution-oriented rules are a greater part of the way of life in Congress than they are in state legislatures,[6] where individual-oriented rules (respect for others, e.g.) are emphasized.

Although the same informal rules are common to all legislatures, their relative weight varies. For example, norms requiring support of political parties are more significant in competitive New Jersey than in free-wheeling California, where norms that require one to keep individual commitments are relatively more vital.

In every group, somebody violates the rules. Legislatures are no exception, and this fact is so widely accepted that there are clear-cut punishments, or sanctions, for violators. The most commonly used sanction in the four states studied by Wahlke and his associates was obstruction of bills introduced by a member who violated the norms.[7] Other sanctions include personal ostracism, mistrust, and loss of political rewards such as patronage and good committee assignments.

[6] Jewell and Patterson, *op. cit.*, p. 376.
[7] Wahlke *et al.*, *op. cit.*, pp. 364–69.

V EXTERNAL FORCES

We turn now from internal factors in state legislatures to external influences that impinge on the legislative process and influence the behavior of legislators. The state legislator plays a series of representative roles: he may alternately represent such external forces as his geographic constituency, his political party, interest groups, or perhaps the governor. The complexity of these various influences means that the legislator can play many different roles in carrying out his constitutional function, and each of these influences should be thought of as an alternative focus of representation.[1]

John Wahlke and his associates have further dis-

[1]For an elaboration of the concept of legislative roles, see Part Four of John C. Wahlke, Heinz Eulau, William Buchanan and LeRoy C. Ferguson, *The Legislative System: Explorations in Legislative Behavior* (New York: John Wiley & Sons, Inc., 1962), pp. 237–376. Chapter 12, "The Legislator as Representative: Representational Roles," pp. 267–86 is the most relevant for our discussion. See also Chap. 16 of Malcolm E. Jewell and Samuel C. Patterson, *The Legislative Process in the United States* (New York: Random House, 1966), pp. 382–410.

It is perhaps worth noting here that we have selected for discussion those role orientations that bear most directly on the legislator's relationship with certain external forces. This by no means exhausts the range of roles that might be of interest to the researchers; for example, see James D. Barber's study, *The Lawmakers : Recruitment and Adaptation to Legislative Life* (New Haven: Yale University Press, 1965) in which he includes a discussion of the manner in which legislators relate to the internal process of the representative body. Wahlke and his associates, *op. cit.*, pp. 3–28, suggest the variety of roles that might be of interest.

tinguished the *focus* of representation (the object of his attention) from the *style* of representation (the manner in which he reacts to the chosen object). A legislator's style of representation may vary, depending on how he chooses to relate to each of the particular influences. The research of political scientists now commonly distinguishes three modal styles of representation: the trustee, the delegate, and the politico. The trustee uses his own judgment and votes on the basis of his principles (or at least says he does when approached by interviewers). The delegate accepts the instructions of others as the basis of his voting and generally feels that his task is simply to determine what is wanted and then vote that way. This sort of legislator might be thought of as a conduit, through which demands are channeled from the external force to the legislature; the trustee might also be thought of as a conduit, but as one that bends and alters possible external demands and largely determines the course of action himself. The politico is a broker of interests who generally assumes both the trustee and delegate roles at times and seeks to reconcile these diverse orientations. The most important distinction to keep in mind is that *style* is taken to mean the manner in which a representative responds to a particular influence: a delegate will probably look for instructions from his district, party, or interest group; a trustee is likely to vote only in accordance with what *he* believes is best for the groups toward which he chooses to orient himself; the politico is a blend of both.

The remainder of this chapter will be devoted to a discussion of the focus of representation—forces that may capture the legislator's attention and exercise some kind of influence over his voting behavior. Among the influences are four major ones: constituency, party, interest groups, and gubernatorial leadership.

CONSTITUENCY

Most of the research on state legislatures falls into two major types: interview projects, in which legislators are asked to describe their perceptions and behavior;[2] and roll-call studies, which examine actual patterns of legislative voting and seek to explain the influences that produce them.[3] The two methods are not mutually exclusive, but often the costs of doing research limit the individual analyst to one approach or the other. In the case of the relationship between constituency and the behavior of legislators, both modes of analysis have produced

[2] See Wahlke *et al., op. cit.,* for an example of a large-scale project in which the legislators in four state legislatures were interviewed with identical techniques, so that comparative analysis could be accomplished. This volume also contains useful bibliography for earlier interview studies. For general references on legislative behavior research, consult Norman Meller, "Legislative Behavior Research," *Western Political Quarterly,* XIII (March, 1960), 131–53 and his later article "Legislative Behavior Research Revisited: A 'Review of Five Years' Publications," *Western Political Quarterly,* XVIII (December, 1965), 776–93.

[3] For bibliography and a discussion of specific research techniques, consult Lee F. Anderson, Meredith W. Watts, Jr., and Allen R. Wilcox, *Legislative Roll Call Analysis* (Evanston: Northwestern University Press, 1966).

findings that are often complementary and substantially increase our knowledge of the legislative process.

Interview research has demonstrated that legislators differ in their orientations toward the districts from which they are elected. Studying four states (New Jersey, California, Tennessee, and Ohio), Wahlke and his associates found that legislators could be classified as either primarily *district* oriented or primarily *state* oriented.[4] Those in the first group tend to put greatest importance on their responsibility to the district that elected them; statewide concerns are secondary. Those in the second group are more cosmopolitan in view, and they express a desire to serve the interests of the state as a whole, even when those interests may not be favorable to their localities. Some legislators are able to maintain both positions simultaneously; but this combination leads one to suspect that on issues crucial to the district, the legislator would probably be motivated by localism rather than by his broader inclinations.

The degree of interparty competition in a district helps to explain this variation among legislators. One plausible hypothesis is that legislators from more competitive districts will tend to be locally oriented, because their re-election depends in large measure on their satisfying local demands. Legislators from competitive districts, knowing that their party label alone will not assure them of re-election, must be more concerned about the specific interests of their districts; but legislators from one-party districts are in less danger from the opposition and can concern themselves with a broader, state interest. It should be remembered, though, that noncompetitiveness tends only to provide a measure of freedom for the legislator; whether he actually develops a statewide interest depends largely on his inclinations. If his own orientation is mainly localistic, the absence of retribution at the polls will not of itself make him broader in his interests.

It is often difficult to separate the influence of constituency from the influence of party, however. In many states (particularly in the Midwest and East) there is a pattern of Republican dominance in the rural and suburban areas, while the Democratic party represents the cities. Where that occurs (e.g., Michigan, Illinois, New York, and Wisconsin) there tends to be a congruence between party and constituency. When legislators represent areas that are not strongly committed to their own parties, Democratic and Republican delegates tend to vote alike.[5]

One way to distinguish between party and constituent influence is to examine the behavior of legislators from districts that are not typical of their parties — rural Democrats and urban Republicans in the Midwest and East, for example — to see if they follow party lines or constituents' preferences. Roll-call voting does indicate that legislators from atypical districts oppose their party's position more often than those from typical areas, apparently in an attempt to provide what they feel is

[4] Wahlke *et al.*, *op. cit.*, p. 288 ff.

[5] David Derge, "Metropolitan and Outstate Alignments in the Illinois and Missouri Legislature Delegations," *American Political Science Review*, LII (December, 1958) 1051–65.

better representation (or safer, politically, for them). Big-city Republicans will be more liberal—and rural Democrats will be more conservative—than their parties' majorities on policies such as those concerning welfare, labor organization, and improved status for minorities. For example, in Illinois and Indiana some Democrats in the southern districts typically oppose policies designed to favor labor unions, racial minorities, and urban services.[6]

An extreme view of this influence of constituency on voting behavior might suggest that the nature of the district somehow determines how the legislator will vote. This is an extension of the notion that Democrats and Republicans from the same district tend to respond to their districts in the same manner, thereby giving similar policy responses in the legislature. To some extent this is plausible. In a competitive district, the members of each political party tend to deviate somewhat from their party majorities, but in the legislature they still maintain their partisan identity even on issues crucial for their constituencies. In other words, a big-city Republican representative is likely to be more liberal than his rural or suburban colleagues, but he would probably still be more conservative than Democrats from the same area.

It seems also likely that the relative size of the district has an influence on voting behavior. Thomas Dye has discovered that members of the upper and lower houses in the Pennsylvania Legislature tended to differ in the responses they gave to roll-call votes on public policy.[7] The logic behind this relationship is this: in state senate districts, the populations are larger and more heterogeneous than in the smaller districts of the lower house. Therefore, a senator may tend to be less localistic and somewhat more cosmopolitan than his colleagues from the lower house. This relationship may not hold for all legislatures, but it does point up one important influence on legislative behavior; namely, that a legislator from a heterogeneous district is likely to behave differently from a legislator from a smaller, more homogeneous constituency.

Thus far, we have been concerned with the relationship between constituency and party where there is a viable two-party system in which each party may expect to gain power from time to time. This situation, of course, does not hold for a significant number of states. There appears to be a general tendency for interparty competition to increase in the United States as the national character of major political and economic issues makes itself felt across the nation. Republicanism is growing in the South; Vermont now elects an occasional Democrat, and so on; however, interparty competition is still lacking in many areas. As a general proposition, we can suggest that the influence of

[6]John H. Fenton comments on these and other party differences in *Midwest Politics* (New York: Holt, Rinehart & Winston, 1966). For some empirical research on constituency differences, see: Duncan MacRae, "The Relations Between Roll-Call Votes and Constituencies in the Massachusetts House of Representatives," *American Political Science Review*, XLVI (December, 1952), pp. 1046–55; and Frank J. Sorauf, *Party and Representation* (New York: Atherton Press, 1963).

[7]Thomas R. Dye, "A Comparison of Constituency Influences in the Upper and Lower Chambers of a State Legislature," *Western Political Quarterly*, XIV (June, 1961), pp. 473–80.

constituency on legislative voting is stronger in states where virtually all members in the legislature are of the same party. Where partisan affiliations are all the same (as in many solid Democratic southern legislatures), the major distinguishing characteristic among voting patterns is likely to be constituency.

One researcher has found that there is in fact a quasi-partisan conflict in the Florida Legislature, where there are fairly consistent policy differences between the rural northern representatives and the delegates who come from the more urban districts around Miami and elsewhere.[8] Similarly, Samuel Patterson's study of the Oklahoma house of representatives indicated that in the absence of party competition in the legislature (virtually all were Democrats when he conducted his study), voting responses of legislators could be explained in terms of constituency differences.[9] Voting on the governor's program was related to the political competitiveness of districts. Districts of higher socioeconomic status tended to be more favorable to increased educational expenditures. Voting on questions of public morals brought differential responses from urban and rural districts. Because voting alignments shifted from one category of issue to another, the constituency factors in voting were not so immediately apparent as they would have been in a simple urban versus rural factionalism; yet, except for several issues of major importance, Patterson concluded that constituency was a basic factor in legislative roll-call voting in Oklahoma.

State constitutions may affect the extent to which legislators devote their attention to local matters. Some states, notably in the South, allow the legislature to enact statutes that affect only one local unit of government, which is specified by name. Other states prohibit local bills, but the same effect can be achieved by using a classification system for cities and counties and then passing general legislation that is based on such a narrow classification that it affects only one municipality. For example, in a state having only one city with a population over one million, a statute legislating for all cities over one million affects only that city. When the Illinois Legislature passes a law designed to affect only those cities with populations in excess of one million residents or makes a special provision for "them" in a bill, there is little doubt that Chicago is being singled out for special treatment.

In southern states that allow the legislature a free hand with local bills, the legislator may devote most of his time to introducing and securing passage of bills such as those adding another registrar in probate to the county court, increasing the salary of county officials, or changing the location of a highway in a village. His role then changes from that of a state official to a local one who is judged by his performance in local functions only.

Hallie Farmer, in her study of the Alabama Legislature, maintained

[8] Malcolm G. Parsons, "Quasi-Partisan Conflict in a One-Party Legislative System: The Florida Senate, 1947–1961," *American Political Science Review*, LVI (September, 1962), 605–14.

[9] Samuel C. Patterson, "Dimensions of Voting Behavior in a One-Party State Legislature," *Public Opinion Quarterly*, XXVI (Summer, 1962), 185–200.

that Alabama legislators concentrate most of their attention on their local bills. As a result, she argued, the governor's legislative program on major public policy was always passed overwhelmingly and with few questions asked, because the legislators could not risk the governor's displeasure. Legislators feared vetoes of local bills and the withholding of patronage.[10]

In some states, the construction of state highways and other public improvements or the granting of state contracts to local business occupy much of the legislator's time. Or patronage in the form of jobs may be politically important. In these circumstances, the legislator's district assumes a saliency for him that it would not have in a state where decisions such as those involving the construction of highways are made by professional engineers in an agency not directly subject to legislative control.

A legislator will direct his energies toward activities that will be favorably judged by his constituents. If the home folks evaluate him on the basis of what he has done for them lately, he will apply himself to that kind of achievement. In a state such as Wisconsin, where there are no local bills and very little patronage of this type, the legislator will be judged on other criteria and will direct his energies accordingly.

In all states, legislators must devote time to running errands for their constituents. As state governments assume more functions, these services become increasingly more time consuming. Although the case-work load of state legislators is not so great as that of congressmen, the demands it places on legislators may be greater because legislators lack the large staffs that congressmen assign to this work. Only California provides its legislators with individual staff assistance in Sacramento and in their home districts. The legislator may literally have to run around to state agencies and then write his own letters from a hotel room to his constituents. Errand running includes helping to arrange entrance into state institutions, obtaining low-numbered or special auto licenses, or obtaining welfare benefits. Numerous requests for assistance are missent to legislators, for many persons have only a vague idea of what the state government does, and they ask their legislators' assistance for matters that are dealt with either in Washington or locally.

PARTY

A legislator's world is filled with competing interests and conflicting demands. Often, no clear answer appears to guide him to an unambiguous choice among several available. Because of the high cost (in time and energy) of gaining all the requisite information and because a legislator must have an eye to the possible political consequences of a wrong choice, he is often anxious to find someone to give him proper

[10] Hallie Farmer, *The Legislative Process in Alabama* (University, Alabama: University of Alabama Press, 1949)

cues, to guide his behavior in areas in which he is not well informed.[11] These cues can help resolve the ambiguity in many decisions he has to make. In the previous section, we discussed constituency as a source of orientation for a legislator; we shall now concentrate on party as a reference group and cue-giving mechanism.

In general, those states in which two-party competition is prevalent on the statewide level will also have relatively active competition between parties in the legislature. If the party in the electorate is competitive, the party in the legislature is likely to be competitive also. There will probably be members of both parties in the legislature, and each party delegation will have some vested interest in maintaining its identity and building up a legislative record. In this situation, party is likely to become an important reference group and an important source of identity for the legislator.

In one-party states, party may have no meaning as such to the legislators, because everyone has the same label. If everyone is, say, a Democrat, then what kind of cues can the party organization give to a legislator? As we have seen, this circumstance is likely to produce *factions* or voting alignments in the legislature that are based on geographic region (Parson's study), constituency type (Patterson's study), or some other characteristic that is unrelated to partisan identification. Another source of intraparty factionalism in a one-party legislature might be personality-oriented splits—as in the separation between Long and anti-Long factions in several generations of Louisiana politics, or the Proctor and anti-Proctor factions in Vermont's Republican party.[12] When any such basis for factionalism occurs within a political party, simple identification as Democrat or Republican loses much of its meaning. Then factional allegiance, the leadership of the governor, constituency characteristics, and interest-group pressures are likely to be the most significant reference groups and cue-giving mechanisms for the legislator. In states such as Tennessee, the few Republicans are so outnumbered by Democrats that partisanship is not considered important by many of the legislators, and minority Republicans are even given committee chairmanships on occasion. Where the minority is hopelessly outmanned, it may enter into a symbiotic relationship with the majority, in which it supports majority programs and is generally cooperative, so that it can get its share of patronage and perquisites. In such cases, partisan identity and party label do not have much meaning.

In striking contrast with the one-party southern legislatures are the competitive, industrial states of the North, East, and Midwest, where

[11] Sometimes the legislator may determine the kind of cues he gets by the way he chooses his reference groups and by the means in which he selects sources of information. See Lewis A. Dexter's article, "The Representative and his District," *Human Organization* XV (1957), 2–13

[12] For some of the background on Louisiana's factional pattern, see Allan Sindler's article, "Bifactional Rivalry as an Alternative to Two-Party Competition in Louisiana," *American Political Science Review*, XLIX (September, 1955), 641–62. The account is revised to account for more recent political events in his *Political Parties in the American States* (New York: St. Martin's Press, 1966), pp. 36–42. For the Vermont pattern, see Duane Lockard, *New England State Politics* (Princeton: Princeton University Press, 1959), p. 13.

parties are the most critical factor in the legislature. Partisanship is most important when Democrats representing low-income groups from metropolitan centers face Republicans representing middle-income groups from suburban and rural areas, and genuine differences in party programs are based on diverse ideologies and interests. The conflict in legislatures is intensified because the district system for apportionment results in overrepresentation of the dominant groups in the party's constituency; thus big-city Republicans and small-town Democrats are underrepresented. Partisan affiliation achieves its greatest proportions when it is supported by deeper cleavages in the society, notably differences in ideology and constituency type.

Between these extremes of interparty competition, and the lack of it, are the less industrialized, urbanized western states and California. In these states there is party competition, but the groups supporting each party are not so clearly differentiated as in the North and East, nor as fluid as those in the South.

Although the constituency basis for each party is critical in legislative behavior, it is important to differentiate between the party in the electorate and the *party in the legislature.* Because the electoral system distorts the relationship between the two, and because there may be little communication between the party in the electorate and the party in the legislature, the party groups within a legislature may be entities quite different from the external party organizations. Even within the legislative parties there are differences in the way legislators perceive the concept of party. For some legislators, party allegiance may simply be support of, or opposition to, party leaders, especially the governor. For others, party allegiance may be support for certain programs or certain ideologies. Still others may perceive party allegiance as support for the constituency groups on which the legislative party is dependent. Where the party in the electorate finds its major expression through a strong party organization, the legislator may listen closely to its wishes, since this organization may control his political career. Where the organization is not very strong (for example, in states where the primaries remove organizational control from nominations), the legislator is free to interpret the demands of the external party as he wishes.

But whatever their perceptions of party may be, legislators differ in their role orientations toward parties. It is possible to distinguish between party men, indifferents, and mavericks.[13] Party men are those who perceive party as important and support their party's program; in competitive states they tend to come from one-party districts and are liable to be "typical" members of their party. Indifferents may or may not vote with their party, but they do not see it as particularly important. Mavericks tend to deviate regularly from party positions; they are likely to come from districts typical of their party and may reflect constituency orientations which deflect their enthusiasm away from party positions.

Whether or not the party is in a majority or minority status in the

[13] For an explanation, see Malcolm E. Jewell and Samuel C. Patterson, *The Legislative Process in the United States* (New York: Random House, 1966), pp. 390–4.

legislature affects legislators' orientations toward parties. A party with a large working majority may permit more deviation on legislative roll calls than a party whose margin is so close that it needs to muster every vote in a partisan contest. Or the need for cohesion may be not as great in the minority opposition as it is in the party that controls the governorship and the legislative program. However, when a party with a minority in the legislature has an incumbent governor, there may be greater pressures for that minority to preserve cohesion in supporting the administration. All these factors obviously change from election to election, so that it is not possible to categorize the degree of partisanship for both parties in each state on any basis that would have validity beyond one legislative session.

Some indication of the relative importance of political parties in state legislatures may be provided by votes on nonunanimous roll calls. Table 5–1 presents the percentage of roll-call votes on which the majority of one party voted against the majority of the other party in a group of selected states. The table indicates that the highest degree of party voting took place in the legislatures of the northeastern states.

Such statistics, of course, do not indicate the relative importance of the issues that divided the political parties. Here one must look at the kinds of issues on which parties took different positions.[14] In competitive states, the issues most likely to lead to parties' voting against one another with a high degree of cohesion are those that pit the interests of the constituency groups against one another (such as the Michigan Democrats' support for labor versus the Republicans' support for business and farmers), those that involve support for, or opposition to, the governor's program (especially budget and revenue measures), and those that involve the institutional interests of the parties themselves (such as election regulations and legislation affecting partisan officer holders). In other cases, partisan roll calls may result from cue-giving mechanisms not perceived by the legislators as partisan.[15] Thus, partisan roll calls on issues such as lady wrestling and dog licenses appear to result from members simply supporting a member of their party on minor issues.

Advocates of "responsible" political parties urge that parties ought to have clear platforms supported by all legislators of that party in order that voters may choose between genuine policy alternatives.[16] Propo-

[14] For several studies of party voting in state legislature, see William J. Keefe, "Parties, Partisanship and Public Policy in the Pennsylvania Legislature," *American Political Science Review*, XLVIII (June, 1954), pp. 450–64; William J. Keefe, "Comparative Study of the Role of Political Parties in State Legislatures," *Western Political Quarterly*, IX (1956), pp. 726–42; Thomas A. Flinn, "Party Responsibility in the States: Some Causal Factors," *American Political Science Review* LVIII (March, 1964), pp. 60–71; and Sorauf, *Party and Representation* (New York: Atherton Press, 1964)

[15] See Wilder Crane, Jr., "A Caveat on Roll-Call Studies of Party Voting," *Midwest Journal of Political Science*, IV (August, 1960), pp. 237–49; and rejoinder by Fred I. Greenstein and Alton F. Jackson, "A Second Look at the Validity of Roll-Call Analysis," *Midwest Journal of Political Science*, VII (May, 1963), pp. 156–66.

[16] The clearest application of this thesis to state legislatures is Malcolm E. Jewell, *The State Legislature: Politics and Practice* (New York: Random House, 1962)

TABLE 5 – 1   **PARTY VOTING IN SELECTED STATE LEGISLATURES,
NONUNANIMOUS ROLL CALLS***

Roll Calls, Majority of Both Parties Opposed

State	Total % such roll calls		%, each party has 80 index of cohesion	
	Senate	House	Senate	House
R. I.	96	96	—	—
Conn.	90	83	—	—
Mass.	82	87	—	—
N.Y.	62	61	32	34
Pa.	64	81	52	56
Pa.	34	43	22	30
Pa.	—	29	—	—
Mich.	56	61	—	—
Ohio	52	40	15	7
Ill.	53	54	15	17
Ill.	—	—	—	—
Me.	—	—	—	—
N.H.	72	68	—	—
Wash.	71	51	9	9
Kan.	—	73	—	—
Ky.	54	41	27	7
Colo.	36	38	6	7
Mo.	23	36	1	9
Mo.	—	—	—	—
Calif.	20	32	—	—
Calif.	—	34	—	1
Calif.	31	49	1	3

*All figures in this table are percentages of the total roll calls in a session
with certain categories excluded from the total. In all states unanimous roll
calls are excluded. For those legislative sessions marked with a dagger, roll
calls with 10% or less of the members (or in some cases, of both parties) voting
in the minority are also excluded. The average index of cohesion in the five
New England states includes only those roll calls on which the parties were
in opposition; for Ohio and Kansas it includes all roll calls listed in the other
columns for those states. Kansas roll calls exclude those with less than 20%
in opposition.

The figures are based on the following sources cited in the footnotes in *The*

nents of this view have looked with favor at a high degree of party
cohesion on legislative roll calls. Yet, in looking at particular circumstances it is often difficult to equate a large number of partisan roll calls
with the importance of political parties as sources of state policy.

For instance, after Wisconsin's 1958 elections, ending twenty years of
Republican dominance, governors of one party faced the opposition
party for four terms in one or both houses. The increase in party
competition resulted in a drastic increase in party roll calls on issue
after issue that, before 1958, would not have been partisan. Yet, each
session, on the most critical issue in the state—the budget-tax measure—the final vote in the legislature witnessed both parties splitting, so

TABLE 5−1 (Cont.)   **PARTY VOTING IN SELECTED STATE LEGISLATURES, NONUNANIMOUS ROLL CALLS***
Roll Calls, Majority of Both Parties Opposed

%, each party has 60 index of cohesion		Average index of cohesion (median of sessions)				Year
Senate	House	Senate		House		
		D	R	D	R	
92	88	95	95	99	98	1931, 1937, 1951
71	77	88	86	87	80	1931−1951
36	56	84	63	82	66	1931, 1937, 1951†
—	—	—	—	—	—	1947, 1949†
—	—	—	—	—	—	1945†
25	30	—	—	—	—	1951
—	14	—	—	—	—	1959
24	43	—	—	—	—	1962†
26	13	67	73	57	55	1935, 1949, 1955, 1957†
—	—	—	—	—	—	1949†
32	26	—	—	—	—	1949−1957
—	—	95	32	71	48	1937, 1951
30	18	83	62	58	52	1931, 1937, 1951†
—	—	—	—	—	—	1945†
—	—	—	—	49	29	1953, 1955, 1957†
—	—	—	—	—	—	1944, 1946†
—	—	—	—	—	—	1941, 1947†
—	—	—	—	—	—	1945−1946†
—	21	—	—	—	—	1955, 1957†
—	—	—	—	—	—	1947−1949†
—	—	—	—	—	—	1957†
—	—	—	—	—	—	1959†

Legislative Process in the United States: Lockard, Jewell, Sorauf, Flinn, Grumm, Young, Buchanan; and on W. J. Keefe, "Parties, Partisanship and Public Policy in the Pennsylvania Legislature," *American Political Science Review,* XLVIII (1954), 450−64; D. R. Derge, "Urban-Rural Relationships in the Illinois General Assembly, 1949−1957" (paper presented at the 1958 meeting of the Midwest Conference of Political Scientists); R. S. Friedman and S. L. Stokes, "The Role of Constitution-Maker as Representative" (unpublished paper).
From Malcolm E. Jewell and Samuel C. Patterson, The Legislative Process in the United States *(New York: Random House, 1966), pp. 420−421.*

that the most important issue of public policy was passed by one group of Democrats and one group of Republicans who voted together against other groups in their own parties. Because divided government is so common in the American states, sometimes the only way to keep the business of state government going is to seek compromises even when those compromises make it impossible for voters to assess partisan responsibility for legislative decisions. American state parties are pragmatic groups with heterogeneous interests. They represent diverse constituencies. The notion of "responsible political parties" along a British or Continental model therefore falls prey to the brokerage function performed by American parties, diluting the party's accountability to the public by injecting constituency and other influences into the legislative process.

INTEREST GROUPS

In addition to a legislator's role relationship to his district and his party, he has a relationship to other groups who seek the enactment or defeat of specific bills. The groups may be well-organized and may employ professional persons (lobbyists) to promote their interests. Lobbyists exceed legislators in number and may surpass legislators in professional competence.

As they differ in orientation toward their districts and parties, so legislators differ in orientation toward interest groups. Wahlke and his associates in their study of four states determined the following three role orientations toward pressure groups:

Facilitators: Have a friendly attitude toward group activity and relatively much knowledge about it.

Resisters: Have a hostile attitude toward group activity, though relatively much knowledge about it.

Neutrals: Have no strong attitude of favor or disfavor with respect to group activity (regardless of their knowledge of it) or have very little knowledge about it (regardless of their friendliness or hostility toward it)[17]

The states differ from one another in role orientations, including their orientations toward pressure groups: Tennessee had fewer facilitators than Ohio, New Jersey, and California, while California had the lowest percentage of resisters. Categories of legislators showed clear separation in pressure group orientations: the best educated and most experienced legislators tended most to be facilitators.

Any shared interest by any group of citizens may be the basis for the formation of an interest group concerning itself with state legislative activity that could affect that group. What is striking about state interest group politics, however, is that state regulations are often so detailed and extensive that innumerable interests may be affected. As a result, state legislators may become embroiled in more intergroup battles than a U.S. representative. In some states, notably Michigan, the legislature is the site for a considerable amount of conflict between labor and management; however, it appears that a large proportion of state group conflict does not include interests that are so well known or visible. More typical are conflicts between druggists and grocers over the right to sell aspirin, between builders and real estate brokers over the right to sell new houses, between engineers and architects over the right to design public buildings, between medical doctors and chiropractors over rights to heal the sick, between wealthy farmers and mar-

[17] Wahlke, *et al., op. cit.,* p. 325

ginal farmers over the standards of grade-A milk, between industrial unions and craft unions, between cities and counties over the distribution of highway aids, between the state teachers' colleges and the state universities over expansion of facilities and establishment of branches. This sort of bifurcation within various segments of the economy means that the legislator is often ill-advised to think categorically in terms of a monolithic "farm vote," or "labor vote," or the like. Diverse lobbyists may pose as the representatives of such segments of the economy and in fact represent only a very small, but perhaps vocal, part of a group. In some states, conflicts between industrial unions and the somewhat more conservative craft unions may make it impossible for a legislator to be a "good man for labor" even if he so wishes.

Although survey research suggests — and most legislators instinctively feel — that party is the most important influence on voting behavior in the electorate, legislators are concerned about the reaction of organized groups in their districts. Small groups who feel keenly about some issue may tip the balance in a contested election; in a competitive district they may influence the results of a general election. Even in a one-party district, they may influence the result of an election — especially in primary elections, because participation in primaries is generally low. A small but determined, well-organized minority may be able to enchance its power by using primaries to dispose of a hostile or uncooperative legislator. No matter how much a legislator may resist interest group demands, he cannot ignore their potential strength.

Group demands are usually presented by lobbyists who speak with legislators in private or at committee hearings and who, if they represent well-organized groups, keep in touch with the legislators' constituents back home. In the late nineteenth century, lobbyists may have bought votes and bribed legislative majorities, and notions of such corruption persist. All states have statutes prohibiting bribery, however, and they are increasing their regulations on lobbying. Wining and dining of legislators by lobbyists is still a fairly common practice, except in Wisconsin which prohibits even that activity; however, picking up the tab for a legislator's food and drink need not be a particularly insidious ploy. Sometimes it simply represents a means whereby the lobbyist can gain access to the legislator long enough to present his case. Furthermore, even Wisconsin law is somewhat ambivalent in the realm of control over lobbyists, since a decision reached by the state supreme court specified that merely accepting money from interest groups was not sufficient proof of corruption; on the contrary, only proof of "ill intent" (presumably an outright bribe) would be deemed illegal. Most states do require some manner of registration and reporting of lobbyists, even though the means for enforcement of pressure group controls is quite often meager or undefined.

It appears that the change from corruption to persuasion is fundamentally a change in political culture rather than in strict legal controls. And the states differ slightly in what their mores will permit. Thus, the difference between Wisconsin's preventing wining and dining and the lavish entertainment provided the Nevada legislators by the gambling interests is a difference in political culture not to be explained simply on the basis of statutes. In all states, however, the lobbyist who can present some solid data to legislators is most likely to obtain a favorable reaction. He will at least have the attention of the representative if he can offer reliable information, perhaps even drafts of speeches that the legislator may deliver and impress his audience with his *expertise*. If the lobbyist can also offer some proof that some folks back home are concerned, the pressure group may achieve its goal.

It is much more difficult to test empirically the effectiveness of interest groups than it is to test the importance of parties or constituencies. A few studies, however, indicate that pressure groups strongly influenced the results of legislative voting. Patterson found that pressure groups determined voting patterns in some labor and welfare issues in Oklahoma.[18] It appears that pressure groups may have greater influence in one-party states where parties do not structure issues. This follows from the proposition that legislative parties will be more cohesive when intralegislative conflict is strong; therefore, the influence of party allegiance will decrease the potential access of interest groups on some issues. It seems likely then, that pressure group politics would be weaker in competitive two-party states than in one-party states.[19]

Even in competitive states, however, many issues are not partisan and may not invoke strong geographic influences, either. In these cases, pressure group activity may have a much more influential role to play in determining the voting behavior of legislators. In one study of Wisconsin, for example, it was found that the majority of legislators responded primarily to two interest groups — groups of bankers competing for branch banks; individual legislators seemed to favor whichever group appeared to be the most powerful in their districts.[20] Interest group tactics are thus more likely to have the greatest impact when party and constituency demands are diminished; when the legislator can be convinced that a group's interest is consistent with his constituency or his party's demands, then he may be easily resolved in favor of the group.[21]

[18] See Patterson, *op. cit.*, as well as "The Role of the Lobbyist: The Case of Oklahoma," *Journal of Politics*, XXV (February, 1963) pp. 72–92.

[19] Robert T. Golembiewski has commented on this relationship in "A Taxonomic Approach to State Political Party Strength," *Western Political Quarterly*, XI (September, 1958), pp. 500–501. Duane Lockard finds support for this proposition in *New England State Politics, op. cit.*, pp. 332–34. For a good discussion of state pressure group activities, see Harmon Ziegler, "Interest Groups in the States," in Herbert Jacob and Kenneth N. Vines, eds., *Comparative State Politics* (Boston: Little, Brown & Co., 1965), pp. 101–47.

[20] Wilder Crane, Jr., "A Test of Effectiveness of Interest-Group Pressures on Legislators," *Southwest Social Science Quarterly*, XLI (December, 1960), pp. 335–40.

[21] We are here emphasizing the more or less "legitimate" demands made by an interest group, and have not dwelled at any length on problems of corruption in state legislatures. The extent to which such irregularities occur is easily exaggerated; however, this is not to gloss over such problems. Readers interested in some journalistic accounts of corruption might consult Paul Simon, "The Illinois Legislature: A Study in Corruption," *Harper's Magazine* (September, 1964), and Trevor Armbrister, "The Octopus in the Statehouse," *The Saturday Evening Post* (February 12, 1966).

THE GOVERNOR

The governor and the administration are another force that is external to the legislature, profoundly affecting legislative decision making.[22] In fact, it has become customary to call the governor "the chief legislator," in spite of the American constitutional principle of separation of powers. It is a fact of contemporary American politics that governors are now judged primarily by their legislative program rather than by their administrative ability, and most voters as well as most state legislators expect the governor to have a legislative program on the major issues of public policy. One author has argued, in fact, that the weakness of the American governor in controlling the administration was a reason for his devoting more attention to legislation.[23]

Constitutional bases of the governor's legislative power include his right to send or deliver messages to the legislature, the submission of the executive budget, the calling of special sessions (sometimes restricted to the subjects specified in the governor's call), and the veto and the item veto.

Political bases of a governor's legislative power include his position as party leader, his use of public persuasion through news media, where he commands more attention than a legislator can attract, his use of patronage for positions, and his role in awarding contracts.

The formal and the political bases for governors' powers vary from state to state. Joseph A. Schlesinger has devised an index ranking the formal powers of American governors in accordance with their budget, appointive and veto powers, and their tenure potential (length of terms and provisions concerning succeding themselves). This index is presented in Table 5-2.

According to Schlesinger's index, the strongest chief state executive is the governor of New York, who alone appoints other officials, has full responsibility for the budget, very strong veto powers, and serves a four-year term with no restrictions on eligibility for re-election. The weakest governors are in Mississippi, North Carolina, Texas, and North Dakota, where they must share budget powers with several others with independent sources of strength, where administrative officials are appointed by other agencies, where they serve for only two years or are not permitted to run again, and where veto power is restricted.

It is much more difficult to rate the political powers of governors, for these powers will vary with the partisan situation or with the ability of the incumbent. Yet the political powers may be more important than the formal powers, and an effective governor may overcome some of the formal restrictions on his position by extralegal means.

A governor in a competitive state who has a majority of members of his political party in both houses of the legislature has the clearest opportunity for legislative leadership. When the legislators are con

[22] The most thorough discussion of state governors is Coleman B. Ransone, Jr., *The Office of Governor in the United States*, (University, Alabama: University of Alabama Press, 1956).

[23] Leslie Lipson, *The American Governor, from Figurehead to Leader* (Chicago: University of Chicago Press, 1939).

TABLE 5-2   A COMBINED INDEX OF THE FORMAL POWERS OF THE GOVERNORS

	Budget powers	Appointive powers	Tenure potential	Veto powers	Total index
New York	5	5	5	4	19
Illinois	5	5	5	3	18
New Jersey	5	5	4	4	18
Pennsylvania	5	5	3	4	17
Virginia	5	5	3	4	17
Washington	5	4	5	3	17
California	5	3	5	4	17
Maryland	5	5	4	2	16
Missouri	5	4	3	4	16
Oregon	5	4	4	3	16
Utah	5	3	5	3	16
Wyoming	5	3	5	3	16
Montana	5	2	5	4	16
Alabama	5	3	3	4	15
Connecticut	4	4	5	2	15
Ohio	5	4	4	2	15
Tennessee	5	5	3	1	14
Kentucky	5	4	3	2	14
Michigan	5	4	2	3	14
Minnesota	5	4	2	3	14
Nevada	5	2	5	2	14
Colorado	4	1	5	4	14
Idaho	1	5	5	3	14
Louisiana	4	2	3	4	13
Oklahoma	5	1	3	4	13
Iowa	5	3	2	2	12
Nebraska	5	3	2	2	12
Wisconsin	5	2	2	3	12
Georgia	5	1	3	3	12
Massachusetts	5	1	2	4	12
Indiana	3	5	3	1	12
Arkansas	5	2	2	2	11
South Dakota	5	2	1	3	11
New Mexico	4	3	1	3	11
Kansas	4	2	2	3	11
Maine	4	1	4	2	11
New Hampshire	5	1	2	2	10
Rhode Island	4	3	2	1	10
North Carolina	4	2	3	1	10
Vermont	2	4	2	2	10
Arizona	2	3	2	3	10
Delaware	1	1	4	4	10
West Virginia	1	3	3	1	8
Florida	1	2	3	2	8
Mississippi	1	1	3	2	7
South Carolina	1	1	3	2	7
Texas	1	1	2	3	7
North Dakota	1	1	2	3	7

From Joseph A. Schlesinger, "The Politics of the Executive," in Herbert Jacob and Kenneth N. Vines, eds., Politics in the American States (Boston: Little, Brown & Co., 1965), p. 229.

vinced that their fates and the fate of their party depend on the governor's fate, they have the strongest motives for supporting his program.
In the absence of this partisan factor, the governor may develop comparable strength by assuming leadership of a faction in a one-party
state. The Long and anti-Long factions in Louisiana and the Byrd
machine in Virginia were examples of this pattern. In other southern
states the governors may be equally strong by assuming leadership of
their own temporary faction. Such governors may be strong legislative
leaders of the group known as "the administration faction," simply
because the opposition is unorganized and is formed by shifting coalitions from one issue to another.

The traditions within states also affect the powers of the governor
quite apart from their formal powers. Thus, it is customary in Tennessee for the governor to designate the leaders of the legislature,
which, in turn, formally approves his "suggestions."

Another contribution to gubernatorial power is his easy access to
valuable sources of information. To gain mastery over a situation, a
governor can obtain and use more technical information and more staff
aids than most legislators can muster. On a matter demanding technical
expertise, the governor may have the resources of whole departments at
his disposal when he makes legislative proposals or sends representatives to legislative hearings to "lobby" for administration programs.
Legislators, even though not convinced of the wisdom of a program,
may sometimes be cowed into acquiescence by a display of technical
expertise.

The governors whose legislative leadership is weakest are those in
competitive states where the opposition party has a majority in the
legislature. Such governors may exercise some negative leadership by
the use and threat of the veto, but their prospects in promoting their
programs will be determined by their skill at the arduous task of bargaining and compromising.

Divided government has been a common occurrence in American
states. There are states in which there has been divided government
more often than there have been governments composed of members
of the same party in both houses of the legislature and in the governor's chair. In the Northeast and Midwest, Democratic governors have
more often been faced with Republican legislatures than vice versa.
This recurring pattern was caused both by malapportionment and by
the heavy concentration of Democratic votes in core cities. Because of
gerrymandered or outdated district maps, the legislature may remain
in the hands of a rural-based Republican delegation long after Democratic governors are being elected from Democratic votes concentrated
in the underrepresented cities. It seems also likely that growth of
Republican strength could produce the reverse situation: an urban-
based Republican governor who must face a legislature elected from
Democratic rural constituencies. In both situations, reapportionment
can have a substantial impact on the distribution of party strength in
the legislature and on the potential conflict between the governor and
the legislature.

CONCLUSION

The distinction between "internal" and "external" forces in a legislature is not always clear-cut. When we consider a political party, we must distinguish between the party in the electorate (meaning a party's voters and its organization) and the party in the legislature. The electorate is primarily external, but it actually becomes a part of the internal process when legislators take their cues from party influences as they make policy choices. A pressure group may also exist outside the legislature but become an active part of the legislative process as it increasingly gains access to decision makers. Therefore, the problem of drawing boundaries around legislative activity is not easily resolved; perhaps it cannot be resolved because the fundamental purpose of representative institutions is to bring external influences into the legislative arena — to cross the boundaries between what is external and what is internal to the legislature. Furthermore, it is through the individual legislator that we study these influences (whether through interviews or roll-call analysis), because he is the official transmitter and carrier of demands, needs, and expectations into the legislature.

VI THE FUTURE OF
STATE LEGISLATURES

Twentieth century America has struck state legislatures with significant impact. It has given the people's representatives districts that are richer, more industrialized, more urbanized, and more complex than could have been clearly envisaged when most legislatures took form in constitutions of the 1800's. A century-and-a-half ago, legislatures were paramount institutions in American government, overshadowing the limited powers of the executives and possessing sufficient *expertise* to oversee the operations of the minuscule bureaucracies of the time. But the executives grew in their powers as the functions of leadership and initiative slowly came to take precedence over the tour de force of legislatures: deliberation, delay, bargaining, and compromise. Bureaucracies grew to immense proportions. They now rank among the largest employers of skill and executive talent — and the big spenders of funds in the execution of public business. But legislatures fell behind in their prestige and powers, so that they now take part in the general "parliamentary crisis" that affects many Western nations.[1] As their responsibilities for public

---

[1] David B. Truman briefly discusses the status of legislatures in the West in the volume he edited, *The Congress and America's Future* (Englewood Cliffs, N.J.: Prentice-Hall, Inc., 1965), pp. 1–2. A Spectrum Book. Chapter I of this volume deals more specifically with this problem as it is related to state legislatures.

103

policy become more complex, as the demands for action become more acute, as government action in all areas of public life increases, the future of state legislatures becomes increasingly a matter of concern.

One major aspect of the problem confronting state legislatures is that they have changed less than many of our other institutions of government. They have not experienced innovations comparable to the reforms in civil service or in local government at the turn of the century or to the reforms in administrative science of the more recent period. Except for the introduction of electric voting machines, they have not introduced any fundamental changes in procedures. As Alexander Heard describes the situation:

State legislatures may be our most extreme example of institutional lag. In their formal qualities they are largely nineteenth century organizations and they must, or should, address themselves to twentieth century problems.[2]

Changes in the social and economic environment of state legislatures increasingly pose a challenge to their capacity to respond effectively. If the legislatures cannot maintain their role in the development of public policies to meet the changing conditions of the century, their characteristic function of distributing important social values in the society may be drained away; their constituents may channel their demands to other levels or agencies of government that are better suited to adapt public policy to their special needs.

When the legislature cannot or will not exploit its own resources for political power, then the conditions within the state may be "power on the loose"—a situation in which another agency has the chance to pick up the loose ends left dangling by the legislature. Some typical beneficiaries of the legislature's default are: the governor, if he is a strong executive who can overcome an indecisive or dilatory legislature; the judiciary, as in the case of legislative reapportionment; the bureaucracy, when administrative decisions substitute for formal legislation; the national government, as it does with social security, interstate highway construction, urban renewal, and various forms of grants-in-aid; or even local government, when municipalities demand authority to work out their problems that have gone unsolved in the state legislature.

Occasionally, two levels of government will cooperate to bypass the state legislature entirely. For some time, national government and city government have combined efforts in urban renewal and housing. The establishment of a cabinet level department for housing and urban affairs, and the institution of new national government activities such as the poverty program and the teachers corps represent explicit attempts to link national and local agencies without the "interference" of state legislatures.

Some of these influences—such as the growth of federal grant-in-aid

[2] Alexander Heard, ed., *State Legislatures in American Politics* (Englewood Cliffs, N.J.: Prentice-Hall, Inc., 1966), p. 3.

expenditures—offer a strong inducement for the states to meet national standards (or "controls," as critics would have it). When the states cannot offer a meaningful alternative on the state level to respond to growing constituency demands, then the initiative for policy determination is lost. To that extent, state legislatures are subject to influences over which they have no direct control. One significant dilemma was the "Indiana Revolt" of 1951, in which a conservative legislature caused the bulk of national welfare funds for the state to be cut off. Faced with the painful alternative of either breaching the gap with an additional $19 million to continue the programs, or dismantling most of the state's welfare establishment, the state eventually had to compromise in order to have the funds reinstated.[3] Where fiscal alternatives are not readily available to the states, such "revolts" against the national government are likely to be more symbolic than effective. Striking as the Indiana Revolt was, no state has followed this path since, because it poses nearly impossible fiscal problems for the states.

In other respects, however, the state legislatures may be more effective in determining their future. Since many programs at the national level have been instituted simply because states were unable or unwilling to assume responsibilities, it would seem that some of the initiative could be regained if the state legislatures were more responsive to trends developing in their constituencies. Formerly, it was widely believed that malapportionment harbored a host of evils in state government, and the question of redistricting consumed much of the energy of political analysts. Now that the courts have largely resolved the question by compelling apportionment of *both* houses of the state legislatures on a population basis, there has been a dramatic increase in concern about the *structure* and *procedures* of state legislatures. Much of this concern is reform oriented.

REFORM PROPOSALS

In the last few years, long-established groups have intensified their interest in state legislative reform, and a number of new groups have been organized to promote reform.

The National Municipal League has long been concerned with state constitutional reform. Its major proposals are presented in its *Model State Constitution*, which provides for a unicameral legislture and the granting of full authority to pass laws and appropriate funds to the legislature. The Ford Foundation has recently awarded a five-year grant to the National Municipal League to extend its investigation of constitutional and other barriers to the effectiveness of legislatures.

---

[a] The "revolt" was considered by Indiana conservatives to be a victory over "paternalism, doles, and subsidies" of the national government. However, this belated defiance of the New Deal ended when U.S. Senator Jenner (R-Ind.) arranged a congressional amendment under which the state requalified for the funds it had rejected. The Indiana law that had precipitated the stoppage of national funds was later brought into conformance with national demands.

The National Legislative Conference, a group of state legislators and legislative staff officials associated with the Council of State Governments, has for some time been concerned with legislative reform. Its reports have advocated abolishing restrictions on state legislatures and increasing length of sessions, compensation, staff, and services.[4]

A newer group, The National Conference of State Legislative Leaders, has assumed greater importance in the last few years. Jesse M. Unruh, the Speaker of the California Assembly, has assumed leadership based on his own experience in initiating many reforms in his own state. The conference is cooperating with Rutgers University in sponsoring a legislative service center and is promoting other reforms intended to increase the status of state legislatures.

John Anderson, former governor of Kansas, has assumed the leadership in organizing a group of nonlegislators who are committed to similar programs. With grants from the Ford Foundation and the Carnegie Corporation, the Citizens Conference on State Legislatures is promoting research and action programs intended to make state legislatures more professional.

Representatives of these organizations, many other civic leaders, and academicians attended a four-day conference on state legislatures in the spring of 1966 under the sponsorship of the American Assembly. The recommendations of this group, under the chairmanship of Chancellor Alexander Heard of Vanderbilt University, reflect fairly widespread agreement among those seeking reform of state legislatures. Here, in part, is the final Report of the Twenty-ninth American Assembly:

The states differ greatly among themselves in their natural settings, their social and economic life, their political party systems, and in their legislative habits and practices. Recognizing these differences, we offer the following recommendations as a guide for continuing efforts by the states to improve their legislatures.

1. In many states, legislatures operate under severe constitutional limitations on their powers. Provisions safeguarding the rights of individual citizens and basic procedural protections to insure the integrity of legislative processes should be preserved. Constitutions should, however, leave legislatures as unhampered as possible, encouraging the development of their own self-reliance. Constitutional limits on the taxing power, constitutional earmarking of revenues, constitutional requirements that bond issues be submitted to popular vote, and other limitations on a legislature's power to appropriate public funds, and to address itself to public questions, should be eliminated.

2. Use of the popular initiative is inconsistent with representative government, except for the call of a constitutional convention. The referendum should not be employed to reverse legislative decisions or to evade legislative responsibility.

3. Enactment of private bills, bills affecting few persons, local and special bills

[4] National Legislative Conference, *American State Legislatures in Mid-Twentieth Century* (Chicago: Council of State Governments, 1961).

should be minimized in state legislatures. The purposes of such bills, where possible, should be achieved through general legislation.

4. Because public problems often transcend state lines, legislatures should organize themselves to communicate effectively with other state legislatures and agencies of government, and be willing to authorize participation in inter-governmental and regional programs.

5. As the principle of "one man, one vote" is applied, innovations in districting policies to improve patterns of representation are desirable. Districting problems vary greatly from state to state and from area to area within states. Creative use of single-member districts and multi-member districts, alone or in combination, may help solve problems of fair representation, especially in urban areas.

6. State constitutions should provide for periodic mandatory reapportionment. When initial responsibility for reapportionment is vested in a legislature, the authority and duty should be placed in a non-legislative agency to effect the reapportionment should the legislature itself fail to do so.

7. Adoption of a unicameral legislature may prove fruitful in some states. A small unicameral legislature may be especially appropriate in states where the cost of legislative operations is burdensome. Apportionment on the basis of "one man, one vote" has removed one of the historical justifications for bicameral legislative systems. In bicameral systems, states should provide, in applying the principle of "one man, one vote," for differing methods or patterns of representation in the two houses.

8. Legislatures should be of a size to make the position of legislators more important and visible. To permit individual participation, effective deliberation, full staffing, and adequate compensation, legislatures should be no larger than fair representation requires. We believe that in many cases in the United States legislatures are larger than desirable.

9. To develop more responsibility in legislative performance, and more independence, legislatures should be continuing bodies meeting in annual plenary sessions, without limitation of time or subject. Legislatures should be empowered to call themselves into session.

Turnover in office in a representative assembly is inevitable. Electorates change, age takes its toll, members seek other public positions. We are not concerned with this normal attrition. We are concerned about well qualified legislators who voluntarily drop out from service because of the frustrations of legislative life.

Since legislatures cannot perform with maximum effectiveness or function in proper balance with the executive branch unless there is continuity of experience among their members, ways should be found to reduce these frustrations. The following recommendations seek to do this.

10. Demands on the time of legislators are mounting in all states. Just as the burdens of legislative service have increased, so should compensation and other benefits. Properly incurred expenses should be fully reimbursed.

11. Legislatures should address themselves to the important problems of campaign costs. Both the Congress and state legislatures should consider adoption of tax incentives such as limited tax credits and deductions, to encourage widespread popular financial support of candidates and parties. We

also urge the exploration of the possibility of government financing of legislative campaigns.

12. Competent professional staff should be provided the legislature, including staff for the leadership, both majority and minority. Adequate secretarial and professional services should be available to members, both in the capital and in home districts when offices are provided there. Where legislative councils exist, they too should be properly staffed. And competent, professional staffs should be provided, on a year-round basis, for at least the most important committees. In addition, legislatures should provide central services, including bill drafting, law revision, legislative library and reference services. Such central services should be staffed by professional personnel employed on a permanent non-partisan basis.

By providing these staffs the legislative branch will improve its ability to develop programs, undertake research, exercise oversight, analyze and evaluate the executive budget, insure effective post-audit, and interpret and communicate its activities. Legislatures should not encroach upon day-to-day operations or upon the responsibilities of the executive branch.

13. State legislators should be provided adequate offices and equipment in the state capital and, where appropriate, in home districts. In addition, legislative committees, especially those with important year-round responsibilities, should be properly housed and equipped.

14. State legislatures should utilize a strong system of standing committees, few in number, with broad well-defined jurisdictions. Committees in both chambers of two-house legislatures should have parallel jurisdiction to permit joint hearings. The committees should, as far as possible, reflect the major functions of state government. Bills should be assigned to committees by subject matter. Where feasible committee memberships should be proportional to the number of each party in the legislature and each party should be responsible for making committee assignments of its members. The number of committees, their jurisdictions and the rules for reference should be determined by a committee on committees. Committees should meet regularly in open sessions, and in executive sessions when necessary, hold hearings, and publish reports when appropriate. All committee decisions should be made in open sessions.

15. To expedite consideration of legislation, devices consistent with adequate opportunity for debate and deliberation should be adopted. These include prefiling, the consent calendar, electronic voting, fiscal notes, and reproduction of documents by modern techniques.

16. Increasing connections between public and private life have led to public concern over conflicts of interest.

Efforts to define and control conflicts of interest have satisfied neither the public nor the legislatures. We recommend:

First, codes of ethics should be adopted, applying to career, appointed and elected public officials, in all branches of state government.

Second, ethics committees or commissions should be created with advisory, review, and investigative functions which should extend to the activities of lobbyists.

Third, all instances of corruption should be vigorously prosecuted.

17. Vigorous party organizations should be encouraged within a state and its

legislature. Well-organized majority and opposition parties contribute to effective and responsible legislative performance. Organization of the legislature should be on a partisan basis in two-party states and the majority party should elect all officers except the officers and leaders of the minority party.
18. Legislative service will become more attractive when the public better understands the importance of legislatures in a democratic society. To improve this understanding, and to enhance the prestige of legislative service, programs should be undertaken to interpret the functions of state legislatures to and through mass media, and educational and civic institutiôns.[5]

ACHIEVING REFORM

To the extent that one can predict the future, it appears that changes will be made in the directions indicated by these proposals. In any event, the trend is toward longer legislative sessions, higher compensation for legislators, increased staff and services. And newer state constitutions have not been so restrictive on the legislature as those adopted in the late nineteenth century. Although it is more difficult to speculate on the nature of reform that may take place in a given state, it seems that the long-term trend is toward increasing the efficiency and satisfactions of the individual legislator by paying him more and giving him more help. A more controversial matter is that of deficit spending, because this issue is normally intertwined with liberal-conservative conflict over the rightful extent of governmental activity. There is a feeling, at least partially in error, that states cannot borrow if the constitution forbids them to do so. The use of the "dummy corporation" and similar devices may eventually be replaced by less restrictive—and more constitutional—means. Constitutional restrictions on the length of sessions and related procedures are gradually giving legislatures a freer hand in dealing with public policy.

A constitution is analogous to a topographical map: it charts the political terrain on which the battles of policy are fought. And it gives strategic advantage to interests that occupy key positions. In the national Congress, those who occupy committee chairmanships and reap the benefits of the seniority system are loath to change the features that protect them and give them power. Although committee chairmanships and seniority are not as important in most state legislatures, certain aspects are sacred. For decades, legislative apportionment systems provided nooks and crannies in which power could be concentrated—power that usually favored rural areas decreasing in population. These areas and their representatives staved off reapportionment until 1962 when the Supreme Court forced them to alter their political terrain.

It should therefore be clear that any alteration in the structures or

[5] The American Assembly, *State Legislatures in American Politics,* Report of the Twenty-ninth American Assembly, April 28-May 1, 1966, Arden House, Harriman, N.Y. (New York: The American Assembly, Columbia University, 1966), pp. 5–9. Chancellor Heard's volume, *State Legislatures in American Politics* was published after this conference.

procedures of state legislatures will have an effect on someone's coign of vantage in the political struggle. Institutional tinkering will generally meet with the resistance of someone whose prerogatives may be impaired in the new arrangement. For this reason, reform or change of state legislatures does not occur simply for the sake of institutional elegance or efficiency, neither of which has proved to be a very strong stimulus to institutional change in state legislatures. On the contrary, our legislatures have proved to be quite durable in spite of their inelegance, inefficiency, and occasional irregularities.

Although interest in the performance of state legislators is greater than ever before, the majority of persons are not particularly concerned about institutions as such. If their attention is turned to state politics at all, it is directed to policy, not structure. Reform is most likely to be achieved if it is related to broader questions of public policy. Municipal reform, for instance, often came about by attracting publicity to the corruption of city governments. State constitutional reform usually comes about only when the constitution creates such insurmountable problems that a broad public will demand change in order to meet substantive problems of public policy. The more fundamental reforms proposed by the American Assembly group and the other groups described here are most likely to be achieved in those states where fundamental substantive problems affect a large number of persons.

Institutional reforms, moreover, are usually supported or opposed on the basis of one's calculations of what effects these structural factors will have on policy outputs. Many of the current reforms are advocated by persons who want state legislatures to do more. Those who believe that governments are already performing too many services and regulating too many activities do not share the enthusiasm for enabling state legislatures to expand the scope of governmental activities. Thus conceived, the abstract rhetoric of institutional reform can serve as an abstract realm in which interests and governmental ideologies jockey for position. Also maneuvering about this realm are the institutional specialists and "good government" people who have a sincere desire to improve state legislatures and who provide legitimacy for reform proposals.

Since much of the debate regarding institutional reform is based on the notion that different structures will produce different policies, it is important to note the paucity of our knowledge here. Reform can have unintended consequences which are unforeseen by the planners, and may nullify the intended good effects of the change. Because of a belated concern for the latent effects of institutional changes, many types of reform in, say, municipal areas were carried through without attaining the expected policy consequences.[6] Likewise, congressional

---

[6] For an insightful analysis of the latent consequences of political organization, see Robert K. Merton's widely-read study, "The Latent Functions of the Political Machine" from his book *Social Theory and Social Structure*, rev. ed. (New York: The Free Press, 1957), pp. 71–81.

reform once drastically reduced the number of committees in Congress, only to find that there was an immediate proliferation of subcommittees! In state government, it was often thought that reapportionment would result in immediate financial benefits to the formerly disadvantaged areas; however, the preliminary evidence indicates that reapportionment of legislatures is not having the consequences hoped for by its proponents or feared by its opponents: rural areas have generally not suffered a drastic decrease in per capita state benefits, nor have urban areas shown a significant increase. In the same way, proponents and opponents of structural reforms may operate on their conception of expected policy results, and their opinions on these matters may be more important politically than the actual facts in the case.[7]

One might expect, for instance, that more professional state legislatures with long sessions, high pay, and adequate staff might place greater value on higher education and therefore be more generous in supporting it. Yet this is a speculation which is still in need of empirical examination by political science researchers interested in state legislatures. Our knowledge is still sketchy concerning the influence of professionalism on legislative policy output.

As another possible consequence of legislative reform, let us consider the position of many advocates of liberal socioeconomic policies who promote reforms intended to result in more professional legislators, on the assumption that greater competence among legislators will result in more liberal legislation. These reform advocates would have miscalculated if a liberal governor faced a conservative legislature whose greater degree of professionalization enabled them to emasculate a governor's program, which a less competent group of legislators might simply have adopted with few questions. Increasing the degree of competence of legislators may have consequences unforeseen by policy-oriented reformers. In general, it appears that reforms geared to improving the efficiency and *expertise* of the individual legislator would have the long-term effect of increasing the powers of the legislature to check the executive and oversee the administration of policy. In fact, those who prefer a resurgence of legislative authority regardless of the immediate policy outcomes have suggested recruitment of experts and proven "watchdogs" to legislatures:[8] others have suggested computerizing the information process of legislatures, so that individual representatives

---

[7] The point here is not, of course, that reapportionment does not have detectable policy consequences. It does, however, take note of the fact that many early claims for reapportionment have not materialized. See Chap. II for a more thorough discussion of this matter.

[8] Although primarily directed to Congress, Lewis A. Dexter's article "'Check and Balance' Today: What Does it Mean for Congress and Congressmen?" is also relevant to legislatures in general. It appears in *Congress: The First Branch of Government* (Washington, D.C.: The American Enterprise Institute for Foreign Policy Research, 1966), pp. 83–113.

could have instant access to vital data needed to provide a counterpoise to the executive.[9]

Even a relatively simple matter such as adding legislative staff may be affected by partisan considerations. If legislative leaders are pitted against a governor of the opposition party, they may not want to depend on sources of information provided by partisan opponents in executive offices; in fact, they may be especially anxious to hire their own assistants to gather information from other sources. If dependable fellow partisans are in executive offices, however, legislative leaders will not be eager to incur expenses for assistance that can be obtained elsewhere in the state government.

The partisan aspect of reform proposals makes it difficult to predict the extent to which state legislatures will be reformed. Nor is it easy to predict the consequences of reforms, once they are enacted. We are developing a new sensitivity to the latent effects of structural change, and recent experience with reapportionment reminds us that institutional change usually does not have an easily envisioned policy consequence. What does seem likely, however, is that the extent of reform in any state will depend on how citizens themselves calculate the alleged policy benefits of reform proposals.

Perhaps, though, the future of state legislatures is less dependent on structural reform than on the larger questions of fiscal capacity. If legislative bodies improve their capacity to respond to changing environmental conditions by altering their apportionment maps and streamlining their procedures, they will still find that many aspects of public policy are beyond their control. State legislatures are not known for their desire to raise tax money to fund new projects, even where the constitution allows them powers of deficit spending and the like. It may be that even after reforms take place, the state legislatures will still not be capable of responding to the complex policy needs of the twentieth century. On the other hand, the state legislatures might gain in prominence if funds available to them were increased, perhaps by means of sharing income tax with the federal government. The Heller plan, articulated by a presidential economic adviser in 1964 and given strong Republican support in Congress in 1967, offered a means by which a portion of the national income tax could be returned to each state. Depending on the restrictions placed on the funds returned, states might generally gain new powers, since they could spend without broaching the politically painful question of taxation.

In any event, a state legislature occupies a key position in adapting public policy to changing social and economic conditions, and it is decidedly important in distributing important valuable goods and services throughout the society. It is the site of many voluble, bitter conflicts among opposing economic and social interests. And it is here that representatives meet for the express purpose of debating issues

[9]See Kenneth Janda, "Information Systems for Congress," *ibid.*, pp. 415–56, for a discussion of the potentialities of computer systems for legislatures. The author also comments on some developments in state legislatures that might be usefully applied to other representative bodies.

and reaching conclusions that are to some degree acceptable to their political constituencies. Their task is made more difficult by a spate of complexities that impinge on the legislative task; however, the most persistent problem facing the legislature is that of producing a satisfactory output of public policy — policy that allocates resources within the state's boundaries. If policies are inadequate to the needs of the constituents, demands may be directed toward other levels or agencies of government, and the stature of the state legislature will be further reduced. Much of the future of state legislatures hinges, then, on their ability to tailor public policy to the changing environment in which they exist.

INDEX

A

Agencies, permanent legislative service (*table*), 68-76
Alabama, 89-90
  reapportionment in, 26, 27
Alaska, 35
Allowances for living expenses, and per diem, for typical legislator (*table*), 51
American Assembly, 109n, 110
Anderson, John, 106
Anderson, Lee F., 86n
Apportionment systems, results of, 31-34
Arkansas, 37
Armbrister, Trevor, 6n, 98n
Articles of Confederation, provision for legislature, 2

B

Baker, Gordon E., 24n, 25n
Baker v. Carr, 18, 24, 25, 26, 27, 29, 32
Barber, James D., 50n, 85n
"Birthright requirements" for legislators, 48
Blair, George S., 1n, 36n
Brady, David, 32n
Buchanan, William, 12n, 43n, 83n, 85n

C

California, 43, 44, 83
Callaway, "Bo," 14
Capitol buildings, official names of (*table*), 56-57
Colgrove v. Green, 25
Committees, 61, 62-64 (*table*), 65-67
Common law, 11, 16
Communist party, 18
Connecticut, 49, 61, 82
"Consent" calendar, 83
Constitution, U.S.:
  Article I, Section, 17
  Fourteenth Amendment, 17
  Republican government, provision for, 2
Compensation of legislators, 50, 51 (*table*)
Constituency, 86-90
Council of State Governments, 106
Crane, Wilder W., Jr., 2n, 32n, 93n, 98n

D

Dawson, Richard, 32n, 40n
Deficit spending, 19-20
"Delegated legislation," 10
Derge, David R., 31n, 46n, 87n, 95n
Dexter, Lewis A., 12n, 91n

115

"Dillon's Rule," 16
Dirksen, Everett, 28
"Dirksen Amendment," 13n
Dixon, Robert G., Jr., 29, 29n
"Double jeopardy," 18
Dragnich, Alexander N., 2n
"Dummy corporation," 20
Duverger, Maurice, 35, 35n, 36, 36n
Dye, Thomas, 32n, 37n, 88, 88n

E

Easton, David, 22, 22n
Edmonds, Douglas, 32n
Educational level of American legislators (table), 46-47
Election systems, 34
"Escalator model" of American politics, 43
Eulau, Heinz, 12n, 43n, 46n, 83n, 85n
Executive:
  as lawmaker, 9-11
  "message power" of, 9
  use of veto, 10
Expenditures of states compared with national government, 6-8

F

Fabricant, Solomon, 8n
Farmer, Hallie, 89, 90n
The Federalist, 3
Fenton, John H., 88n
Ferguson, LeRoy C., 12n, 43n, 83n, 85n
"Filibuster," 81-82
Fjelstad, Ralph S., 34, 61n
Flinn, Thomas A., 93
Florida, 37, 89
Ford Foundation, 61, 105, 106
Fortson v. Dorsey, 31
Fourteenth Amendment, 17
Friedman, Robert S., 32n, 95

G

Georgia, 14, 31, 37
Gitlow, Benjamin, 18
Gold, David, 46n
Golembiewski, Robert T., 40n, 98n
Goodman, W. I., 17n
Governor, 99-102
  powers of (table), 100
Greenstein, Fred I., 93n

Group norms, 83-84
Grumm, John G., 95n

H

Hamilton, H. D., 29n
Havens, Murray, 32n
Heard, Alexander, 104, 104n, 106
Hearings and standing committees, legislative procedure (table), 62-64
Heller plan, 112
Hofferbert, Richard, 32n
Hofstadter, Richard, 4n
Hyneman, Charles S., 48, 49n

I

Illinois, 19, 89
"Indiana Revolt," 105n
Initiative, 11
Interest groups, 96-98

J

Jackson, Alton F., 93n
Jackson, Andrew, 4
Jacksonian Democracy, 4, 11
Jacob, Herbert, 10n, 37n, 38n, 40n, 98n, 100n
Janda, Kenneth, 112n
Jewell, Malcolm E., 1n, 33, 33n, 40, 40n, 42, 45, 46n, 49n, 61n, 84, 85n, 92n, 93n, 95n

K

Keefe, William J., 1n, 2n, 93n, 95n
Key, V. O., Jr., 4n, 23, 23n, 34, 35n, 43n
"King Caucus," 4
Klain, Maurice, 36

L

Labor force, occupations of (table), 45
Legislative Reorganization Act of 1946, 65
Legislative responsibility and turnover, 52-54
Legislative service agencies, 68-76
Legislators:
  educational level of (table), 46-47

numbers, terms, party affiliations (table), 58-60
occupational level of, 47
occupations of fathers (table), 45
occupations of fathers, legislators themselves, senators, and labor force (table), 45
political socialization of, 48
realized compensation in salary (table), 51
residence in district (table), 44
service agencies for (table), 68-76
Legislatures:
and changing society, 21-23
corruption in, 4-5
and direct election of senators, 4
functions of, 1, 9-21
administrative, 11-13
constituent, 13
electoral, 13
investigatory, 14-15
judicial, 13
lawmaking, 15-21
historical trends in, 2-9
names of (table), 56-57
party control and competition (table), 41-42
procedural rules in, 77-83
procedure: standing committees and hearings (table), 62-64
sessions, 77, 78-80 (table)
Lipson, Leslie, 99n
Lockard, Duane, 38, 38n, 49, 49n
Louisiana, 11, 91, 101
Lucas v. Colorado General Assembly, 27

M

McCarthy, Joseph, 35
McClellan-Kennedy investigations, 15
Maddox, Lester, 14
Madison, James, 3
Maine, 66, 82
Manvel, Allen D., 17n
Maryland, 30
Massachusetts, 29, 66, 67, 77, 82
Matthews, Donald R., 45, 45n, 47n
Maxwell, James A., 5n, 8n, 20, 16n
Meller, Norman, 86n
Merton, Robert K., 110
Michigan, 19, 35
Minnesota, 35, 61
Mississippi, 99
Mitau, G. Theodore, 17n, 20n, 61n
Mitchell, William C., 22n

Model State Constitution, 105
Montana, 35
Mosher, Frederick C., 8n

N

Names (official) of states, legislative bodies, and capitol buildings (table), 56-57
National Legislative Conference, 106, 106n
National Municipal League, 105
Nebraska, 55
New England, 49
New Hampshire, 50
New Jersey, 43, 61, 82, 83
New York, 50, 67, 99
North, Barbara, 36n
North, Robert, 36n
North Carolina, 82, 99
North Dakota, 99

O

Occupations:
of fathers of legislators (table), 45
of legislators' fathers, legislators themselves, senators, and labor force (table), 45
Official names of states, legislative bodies, capitol buildings (table), 56-57
Ogul, Morris S., 1n, 2n
Ohio, 43, 83
Oklahoma, 89
Oregon, 37
One-party control of state legislatures (table), 41
Owen, I., 20n

P

Parsons, Malcolm G., 89
Party, 90-96
affiliations of legislators (table), 58-60
"responsibility" of, 93-96
competition, 39, 41-42 (table)
control (table), 41
primaries, 43
rotation agreements, 50
voting, 94-95 (table)
Patterson, Samuel C., 1n, 32n, 40, 45, 48n, 49n, 52, 61n, 64, 65n, 89, 89n, 92n, 85n, 98n
Pennsylvania, 48, 88
Per diem and living expenses allowances for typical legislator (table), 51

"Plural executive," 4
Poland, Orville F., 8n
Prendergast, William B., 33n
Pre-primary convention, 44
Prescott, F. W., 10n
"Presidential Republicanism," 34
primary elections, 34-36
  closed, 34
  open, 35
  runoff, 35-36
"Procedural guarantees," (in U.S., Constitution), 18
Procedure, legislative (table), 62-64

R

Ranney, Austin, 40n
Ransone, Coleman B., Jr., 99n
"Readings" (of bills), 81
Reapportionment:
  background of, 24-28
  problems of, 28-31
Referendum, 11
Reform proposals, 105-109
Reynolds v. Sims, 26, 27, 36
"Right to work" laws, 20
Robinson, James A., 32n, 40n, 43n
Roche, John, 18
Roll-call analysis, 86
Roll calls, nonunanimous, party voting in (table), 94-95
Rossiter, Clinton, 3n

S

Schaller, L. E., 17n
Schlesinger, Joseph A., 10n, 40n, 99, 100n
Schubert, Glendon, 31n
Senators, U.S., occupations of (table), 45
Service agencies, permanent, for legislators (table), 68-76
Sessions (legislative), 77, 78-80
"Short roll call," 83
Simon, Paul, 98n
Sindler, Allan, 91n
Smothers, Frank, 64n, 76n, 80n
Social change and state legislatures, 21-23
Social mobility, 44
Socioeconomic status, 44
Sorauf, Frank, 45, 48, 48n, 88n, 93n
Speaker (of lower house), 65
"Split session," 77

Sprague, John D., 46n
Staff services, 67
Standing, William H., 43n
Standing committees and hearings, legislative procedure (table), 62-64
States, official names (table), 56-57
Stokes, S. L., 95
Supreme Court, 17, 49

T

Tennessee, 14, 43, 47, 83, 91
Tenure and turnover, 48-50
Terms of legislators (table), 58-60
Texas, 99
Truman, David B., 103n

U

Unruh, Jesse M., 67, 106
Utah, 35

V

Vasey, Wayne, 8n
Vermont, 91
Veto, 82
Vines, Kenneth N., 10n, 38n, 40n, 98n, 100n
Virginia, 82
Voting, party, in nonunanimous roll calls (table), 94-95

W

Wahlke, John C., 2n, 12n, 43n, 44, 45, 45n, 48n, 83, 83n, 84, 85n, 86n, 87n
Wallace, George, 35
Warren, Earl, 18, 26
Washington, 66
"WASP's," 48
Watts, Meredith W., 86n
Wesberry v. Sanders, 30
Wheare, K. C., 5
Wilcox, Allen R., 86n
Wisconsin, 19, 29, 67, 77, 97-98
Wright v. Rockefeller, 31

Z

Ziegler, Harmon, 98n